Contents

About *Math Centers, Grades 3–4* 2

Making a File Folder Center 3

Center Checklist 4

Money Match (value of coins and bills; calculating sums of money) 5

Time Marches On (elapsed time) 23

Fill It Up! (measurement, capacity) 37

Number Square Puzzler (computation) 53

Read a Graph (reading bar, line, and circle graphs) 69

Make a Graph (use data to make bar, line, and circle graphs) 81

How Many Combinations? (data analysis and probability) 93

Name That Part! (fractions and decimals) 103

Plotting a Picture (ordered pairs) 121

What's My Rule? (function tables) 131

Analyze the Data (finding range, mode, median) 141

Perimeter and Area (calculating perimeter and area) 153

Transformations (identify how shapes are transformed—turned, slid, flipped) 163

Pattern Puzzles (number patterns) 171

Solid Shapes (count faces, edges, vertexes of solid shapes) 181

Answer Key 189

About Math Centers
Grades 3–4

What's Great About This Book

Centers are a wonderful, fun way for students to practice important skills. The 15 centers in this book are self-contained and portable. Students may work at a desk, table, or even on the floor. Once you've made the centers, they're ready to use any time.

What's in This Book

Teacher direction page
includes a description of the student task

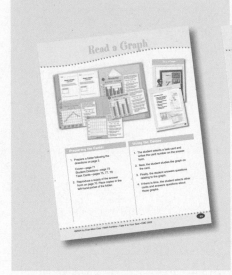

Full-color materials
needed for the center

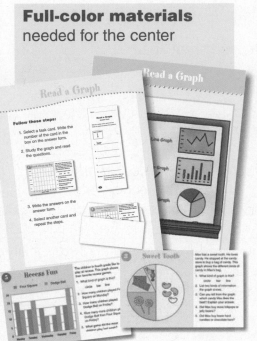

Reproducible answer forms

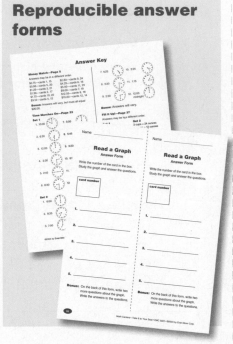

How to Use the Centers

The centers are intended for skill practice, not to introduce skills. It is important to model the use of each center before students do the task independently.

Questions to Consider:

- Will students select a center, or will you assign the centers?
- Will there be a specific block of time for centers, or will the centers be used throughout the day?
- Where will you place the centers for easy access by students?
- What procedure will students use when they need help with the center tasks?
- Where will students store completed work?
- How will you track the tasks and centers completed by each student?

Math Centers—Take It to Your Seat • EMC 3022 • ©2004 by Evan-Moor Corp.

Making a File Folder Center

Materials

- folder with pockets
- envelopes or plastic self-locking bags
- marking pens and pencils
- two-sided tape

Folder cover

Folder back cover
Student Direction page

Folder centers are easily stored in a box or file crate. Students take a folder to their desks to complete the task.

Steps to Follow

1. Laminate the cover. Tape it to the front of the folder.

2. Laminate the student direction page. Tape it to the back of the folder.

3. Place answer forms, writing paper, and any other supplies in the left-hand pocket.

4. Laminate the task cards. Place each set of cards in a labeled envelope or plastic self-locking bag. Place the envelopes and sorting mat (if required for the center) in the right-hand pocket.

Center Checklist

Student Names

Centers

Money Match													
Time Marches On													
Fill It Up!													
Number Square Puzzler													
Read a Graph													
Make a Graph													
How Many Combinations?													
Name That Part!													
Plotting a Picture													
What's My Rule?													
Analyze the Data													
Perimeter and Area													
Transformations													
Puzzle Patterns													
Solid Shapes													

Money Match

Preparing the Center

1. Prepare a folder following the directions on page 3.

   Cover—page 7
   Student Directions—page 9
   Money Cards—pages 11–21

2. Reproduce a supply of the answer form on page 6. Place copies in the left-hand pocket of the folder.

Using the Center

1. The student takes the envelope of money cards and an answer form, and then matches the three cards that represent the same amount of money.

2. Next, the student writes the amount of money (sum) on the first line and the numbers of the two money cards on the next two lines.

3. Finally, the student repeats the task with the remaining cards.

Money Match

Match three cards that show the same amount of money.

Amount (sum)	Cards		Amount (sum)	Cards	
$ ___ . ___	___ ___ ___		$ ___ . ___	___ ___ ___	
$ ___ . ___	___ ___ ___		$ ___ . ___	___ ___ ___	
$ ___ . ___	___ ___ ___		$ ___ . ___	___ ___ ___	
$ ___ . ___	___ ___ ___		$ ___ . ___	___ ___ ___	
$ ___ . ___	___ ___ ___		$ ___ . ___	___ ___ ___	
$ ___ . ___	___ ___ ___		$ ___ . ___	___ ___ ___	

Bonus: Draw or write three ways to show $20.00.

Money Match

Math Centers—Take It to Your Seat • EMC 3022 • ©2004 by Evan-Moor Corp.

Money Match

Follow these steps:

1. Take the envelope of money cards and an answer form.

2. Match 3 cards that show the same amount of money.

 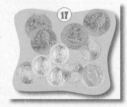

3. Write the money amount (sum) on the first line of the answer form.

4. Write the numbers of the two cards that match that amount on the next two lines.

5. Repeat with the other cards.

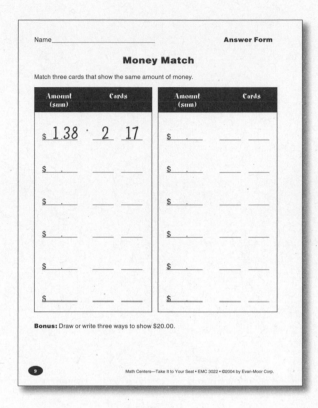

Math Centers—Take It to Your Seat • EMC 3022 • ©2004 by Evan-Moor Corp.

$0.75

$0.98

$1.25

$1.38

$1.72

$3.12

Money Match

EMC 3022
©2004 by Evan-Moor Corp.

Money Match

EMC 3022
©2004 by Evan-Moor Corp.

Money Match

EMC 3022
©2004 by Evan-Moor Corp.

Money Match

EMC 3022
©2004 by Evan-Moor Corp.

Money Match

EMC 3022
©2004 by Evan-Moor Corp.

Money Match

EMC 3022
©2004 by Evan-Moor Corp.

$2.80

$4.25

$5.93

$9.00

$12.55

$15.00

Money Match

Money Match

Money Match

Money Match

Money Match

Money Match

1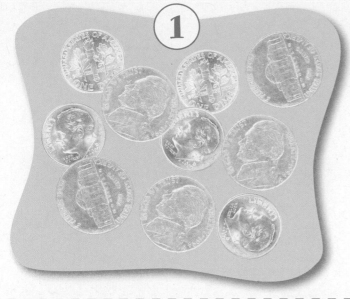

2

3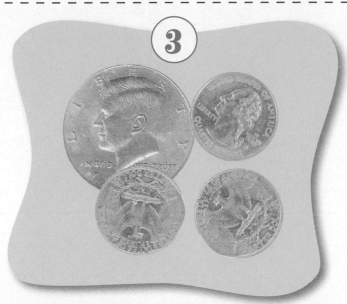

4

5

6

Money Match

EMC 3022
©2004 by Evan-Moor Corp.

Money Match

EMC 3022
©2004 by Evan-Moor Corp.

Money Match

EMC 3022
©2004 by Evan-Moor Corp.

Money Match

EMC 3022
©2004 by Evan-Moor Corp.

Money Match

EMC 3022
©2004 by Evan-Moor Corp.

Money Match

EMC 3022
©2004 by Evan-Moor Corp.

7

8

9

10

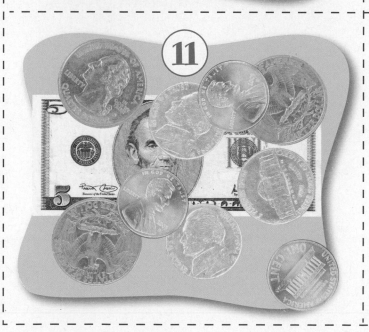

11

12

Money Match

EMC 3022
©2004 by Evan-Moor Corp.

Money Match

EMC 3022
©2004 by Evan-Moor Corp.

Money Match

EMC 3022
©2004 by Evan-Moor Corp.

Money Match

EMC 3022
©2004 by Evan-Moor Corp.

Money Match

EMC 3022
©2004 by Evan-Moor Corp.

Money Match

EMC 3022
©2004 by Evan-Moor Corp.

Money Match

Money Match

Money Match

Money Match

Money Match

Money Match

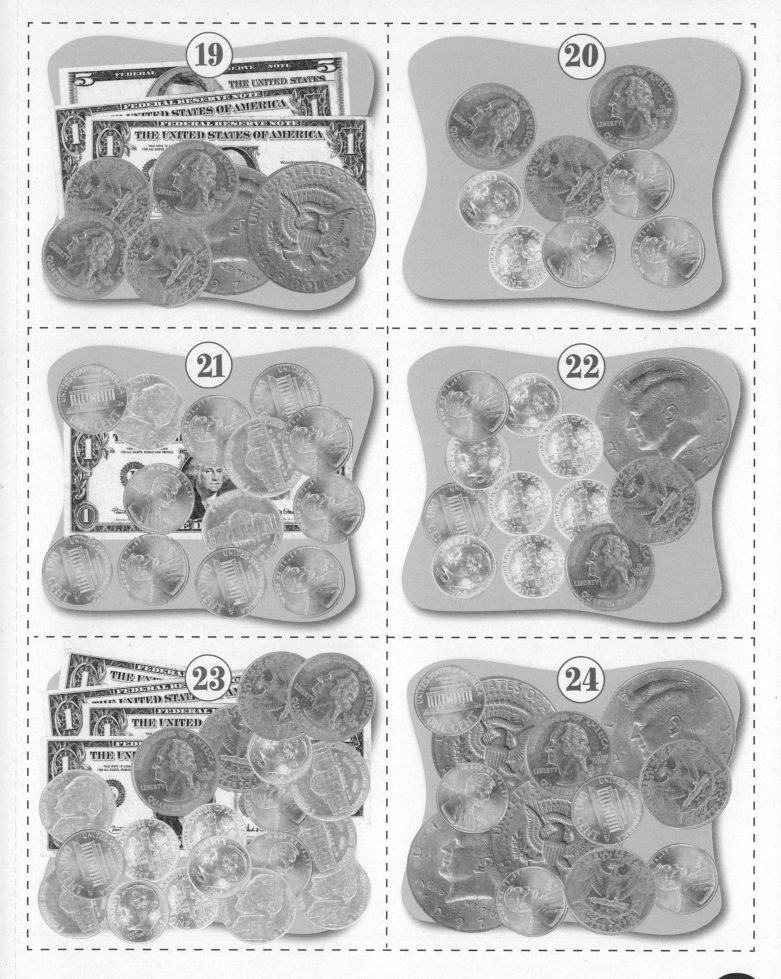

Money Match

Money Match

Money Match

Money Match

Money Match

Money Match

Time Marches On

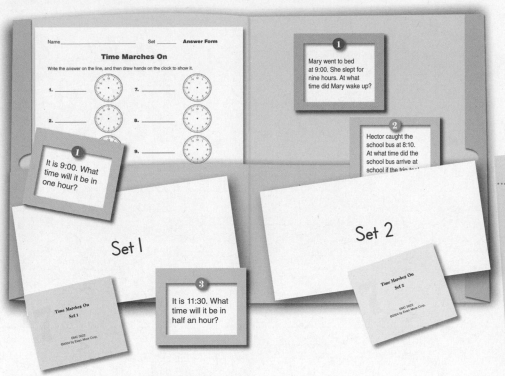

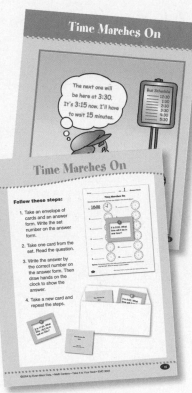

Preparing the Center

1. Prepare a folder following the directions on page 3.

   Cover—page 25
   Student Directions—page 27
   Task Cards—pages 29–35

2. Reproduce a supply of the answer form on page 24. Place copies in the left-hand pocket of the folder.

Using the Center

1. The student selects an envelope of task cards and writes the set number on the answer form.

2. Next, the student takes a card and reads the task. The student writes the answer, and then draws hands on the clockface to show the answer.

3. The student completes all 12 cards.

Time Marches On

Write the answer on the line, and then draw hands on the clock to show it.

1. _____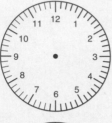

2. _____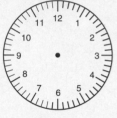

3. _____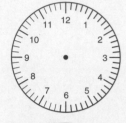

4. _____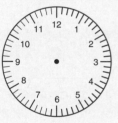

5. _____

6. _____

7. _____

8. _____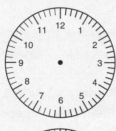

9. _____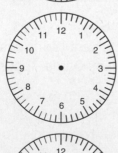

10. _____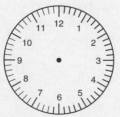

11. _____

12. _____

Bonus: On the back of this form, write a word problem about how many hours you slept last night. Write the answer to your problem.

Follow these steps:

1. Take a set of cards and an answer form. Write the set number on the answer form.

2. Take one card from the set. Read the question.

3. Write the answer by the correct number on the answer form. Then draw hands on the clock to show the answer.

4. Take a new card and repeat the steps.

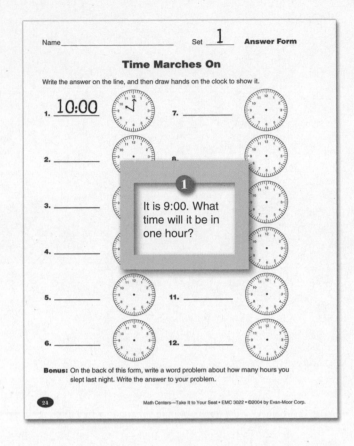

1

It is 9:00. What time will it be in one hour?

2

It is 6:00. What time will it be in half an hour?

3

It is 11:30. What time will it be in half an hour?

4

It is 2:15. What time will it be in fifteen minutes?

5

It is 3:45. What time was it one hour ago?

6

It is 10:00. What time was it an hour and a half ago?

Time Marches On

Set 1

EMC 3022
©2004 by Evan-Moor Corp.

Time Marches On

Set 1

EMC 3022
©2004 by Evan-Moor Corp.

Time Marches On

Set 1

EMC 3022
©2004 by Evan-Moor Corp.

Time Marches On

Set 1

EMC 3022
©2004 by Evan-Moor Corp.

Time Marches On

Set 1

EMC 3022
©2004 by Evan-Moor Corp.

Time Marches On

Set 1

EMC 3022
©2004 by Evan-Moor Corp.

7

It is 7:30. What time was it two and a half hours ago?

8

It is 6:15. What time was it half an hour ago?

9

It is 3:00. What time will it be in 20 minutes?

10

It is 12:00. What time will it be in six hours?

11

It is 1:20. What time was it five minutes ago?

12

It is 8:40. What time will it be in twenty minutes?

Time Marches On

Set 1

Time Marches On

Set 1

Time Marches On

Set 1

Time Marches On

Set 1

Time Marches On

Set 1

Time Marches On

Set 1

1

Mary went to bed at 9:00. She slept for nine hours. At what time did Mary wake up?

2

Hector caught the school bus at 8:10. At what time did the school bus arrive at school if the trip took 25 minutes?

3

Jimmy's birthday party lasted for $5\frac{1}{2}$ hours. If the party started at 1:30, at what time did it end?

4

Tonya spent three hours cleaning her bedroom. If she started at 3:20, at what time did she finish?

5

It took Mother two hours to bake cookies for the bake sale at church. She finished the cookies at 2:25. At what time did she start baking the cookies?

6

It takes Ali 25 minutes to walk from his house to the ball field. If he has to be at the field by 2:30, at what time should he leave home?

Time Marches On

Set 2

EMC 3022
©2004 by Evan-Moor Corp.

Time Marches On

Set 2

EMC 3022
©2004 by Evan-Moor Corp.

Time Marches On

Set 2

EMC 3022
©2004 by Evan-Moor Corp.

Time Marches On

Set 2

EMC 3022
©2004 by Evan-Moor Corp.

Time Marches On

Set 2

EMC 3022
©2004 by Evan-Moor Corp.

Time Marches On

Set 2

EMC 3022
©2004 by Evan-Moor Corp.

7

It was 2:15 when the movie started. It lasted for 2 hours and 10 minutes. At what time did the movie end?

8

It is 5:45. I have been working on my homework for 2 hours and 15 minutes. At what time did I start my homework?

9

Connie spent three hours with her grandma last Sunday. She arrived at Grandma's house at 11:30. At what time did she leave?

10

Max can run from his house to the park in 14 minutes. If he leaves his house at 3:10, at what time will he reach the park?

11

The car trip took us 5 hours and 15 minutes. If we left at 8:00, at what time did we reach our destination?

12

It is 12:00 noon. What time will it be in twelve hours?

Time Marches On

Set 2

EMC 3022
©2004 by Evan-Moor Corp.

Time Marches On

Set 2

EMC 3022
©2004 by Evan-Moor Corp.

Time Marches On

Set 2

EMC 3022
©2004 by Evan-Moor Corp.

Time Marches On

Set 2

EMC 3022
©2004 by Evan-Moor Corp.

Time Marches On

Set 2

EMC 3022
©2004 by Evan-Moor Corp.

Time Marches On

Set 2

EMC 3022
©2004 by Evan-Moor Corp.

Fill It Up!

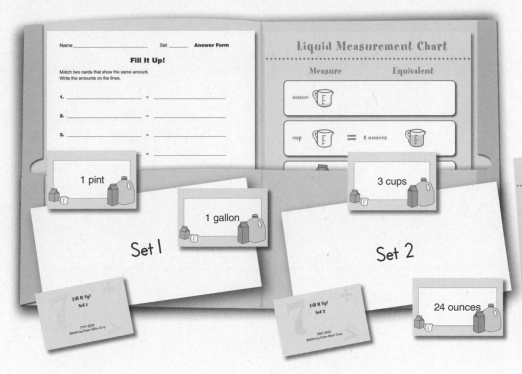

Preparing the Center

1. Prepare a folder following the directions on page 3.

   Cover—page 39
   Student Directions—page 41
   Liquid Measurement Chart—page 43
   Task Cards—pages 45–51

2. Reproduce a supply of the answer form on page 38. Place copies in the left-hand pocket of the folder.

Using the Center

1. The student selects an envelope of task cards and writes the set number on the answer form.

2. Next, the student uses the Liquid Measurement Chart to match two cards that show an equivalent amount. Then the student writes the two amounts on the answer form.

3. Finally, the student repeats the steps with the remaining cards.

Fill It Up!

Match two cards that show the same amount.
Write the amounts on the lines.

1. _____ = _____

2. _____ = _____

3. _____ = _____

4. _____ = _____

5. _____ = _____

6. _____ = _____

7. _____ = _____

8. _____ = _____

Bonus: Write another way of showing the amount in one gallon.

40

Fill It Up!

Follow these steps:

1. Take a set of cards and an answer form. Write the set number on the answer form.

2. Look at the cards. Match two cards that show the same amount. Use the Liquid Measurement Chart to help you.

3. Continue to match cards until you have made 8 pairs.

4. Write the amounts of each pair on the lines.

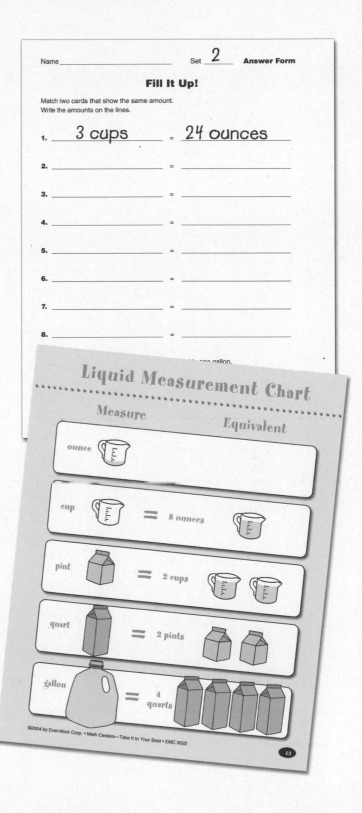

Name _____ Set **2** Answer Form

Fill It Up!

Match two cards that show the same amount.
Write the amounts on the lines.

1. _____ 3 cups _____ = _____ 24 ounces _____

2. _____ = _____

3. _____ = _____

4. _____ = _____

5. _____ = _____

6. _____ = _____

7. _____ = _____

8. _____ = _____

Liquid Measurement Chart

Measure		Equivalent
ounce		
cup	=	8 ounces
pint	=	2 cups
quart	=	2 pints
gallon	=	4 quarts

©2004 by Evan-Moor Corp. • Math Centers—Take It to Your Seat • EMC 3022

Liquid Measurement Chart

Measure		Equivalent

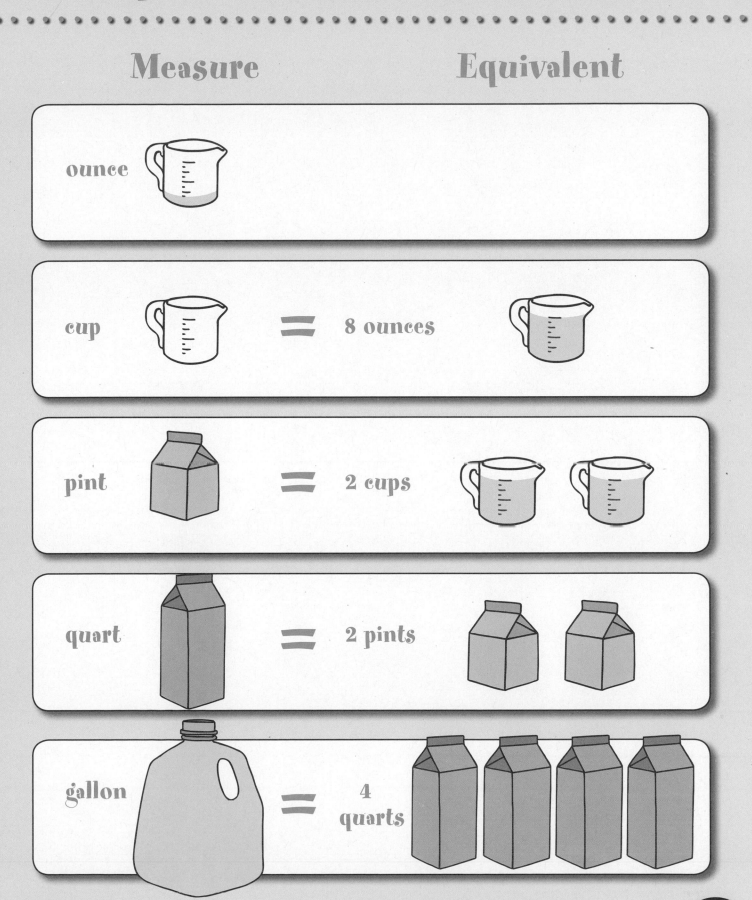

ounce

cup = 8 ounces

pint = 2 cups

quart = 2 pints

gallon = 4 quarts

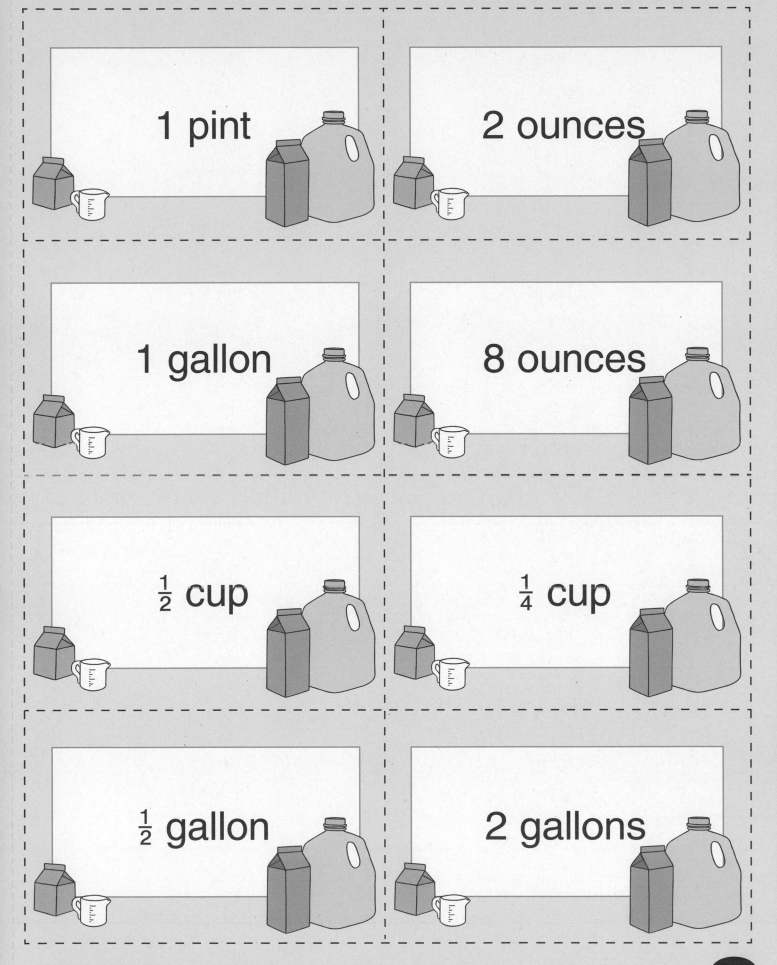

1 pint

2 ounces

1 gallon

8 ounces

$\frac{1}{2}$ cup

$\frac{1}{4}$ cup

$\frac{1}{2}$ gallon

2 gallons

Fill It Up!

Set 1

Fill It Up!

Set 1

Fill It Up!

Set 1

Fill It Up!

Set 1

Fill It Up!

Set 1

Fill It Up!

Set 1

Fill It Up!

Set 1

Fill It Up!

Set 1

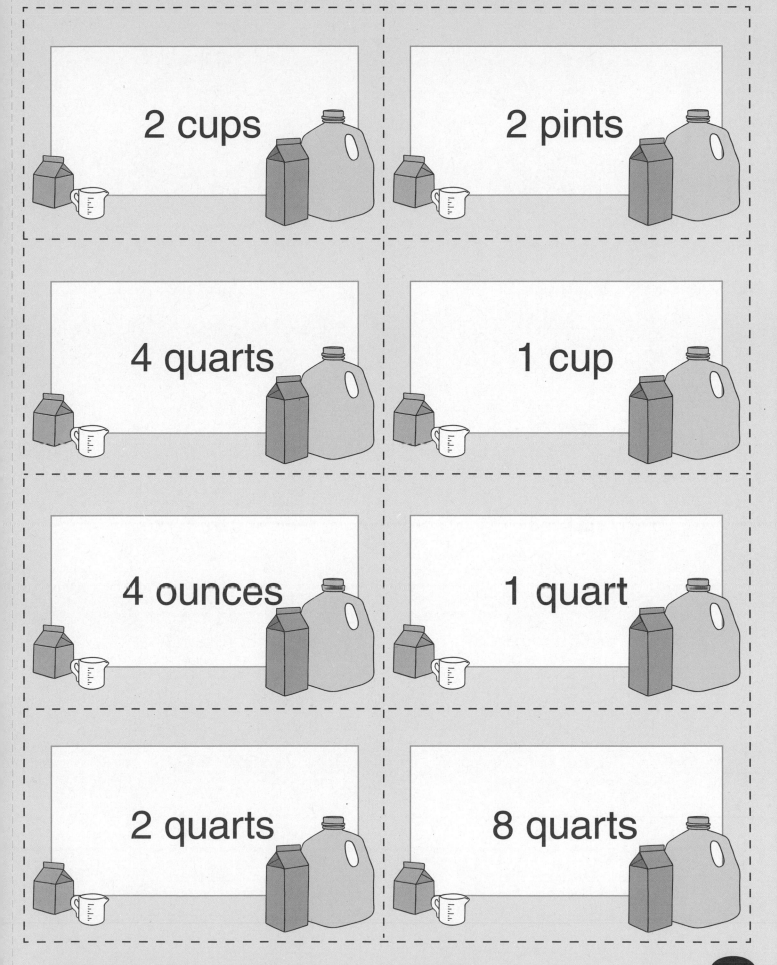

2 cups

2 pints

4 quarts

1 cup

4 ounces

1 quart

2 quarts

8 quarts

Fill It Up!

Set 1

Fill It Up!

Set 1

Fill It Up!

Set 1

Fill It Up!

Set 1

Fill It Up!

Set 1

Fill It Up!

Set 1

Fill It Up!

Set 1

Fill It Up!

Set 1

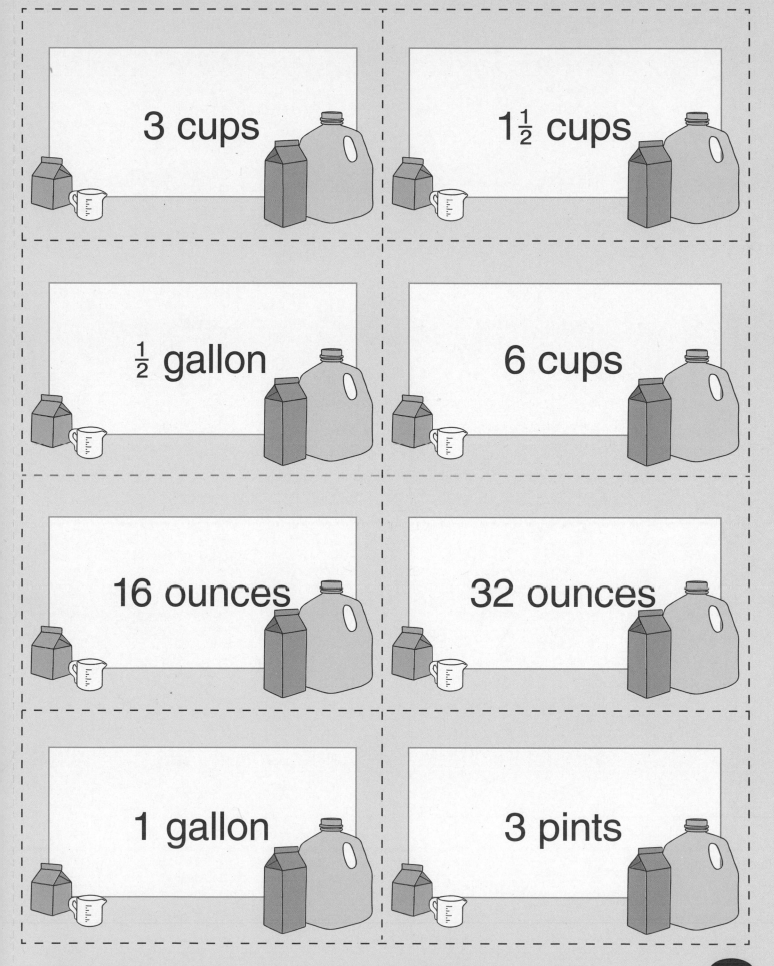

3 cups

1½ cups

½ gallon

6 cups

16 ounces

32 ounces

1 gallon

3 pints

Fill It Up!

Set 2

Fill It Up!

Set 2

Fill It Up!

Set 2

Fill It Up!

Set 2

Fill It Up!

Set 2

Fill It Up!

Set 2

Fill It Up!

Set 2

Fill It Up!

Set 2

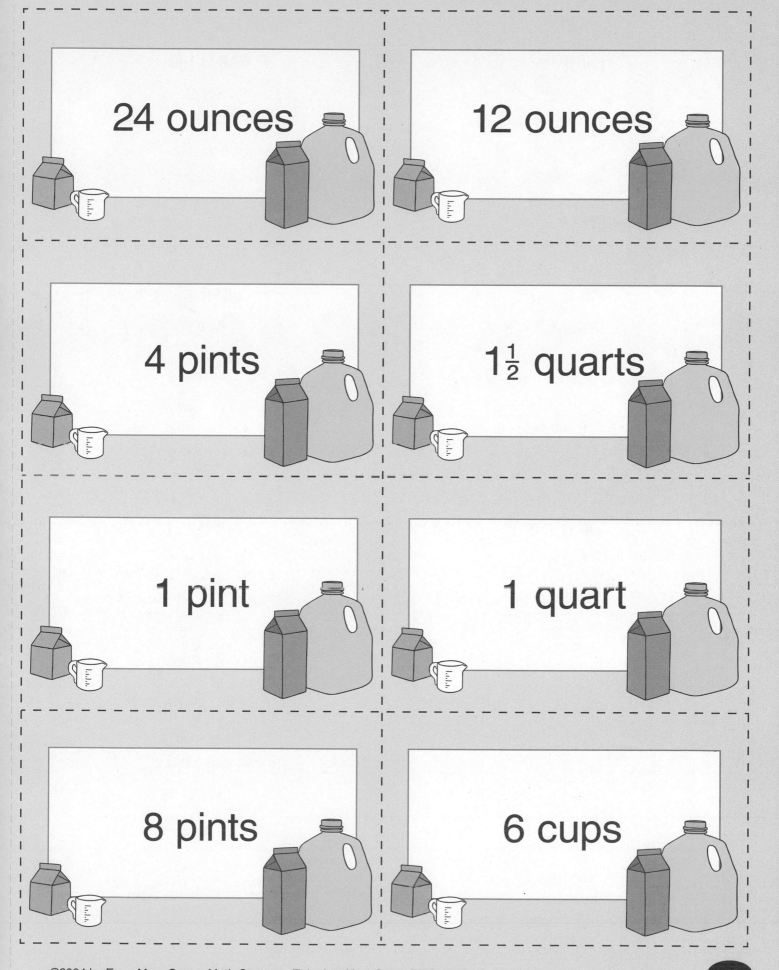

24 ounces

12 ounces

4 pints

1½ quarts

1 pint

1 quart

8 pints

6 cups

Fill It Up!

Set 2

Fill It Up!

Set 2

Fill It Up!

Set 2

Fill It Up!

Set 2

Fill It Up!

Set 2

Fill It Up!

Set 2

Fill It Up!

Set 2

Fill It Up!

Set 2

Number Square Puzzler

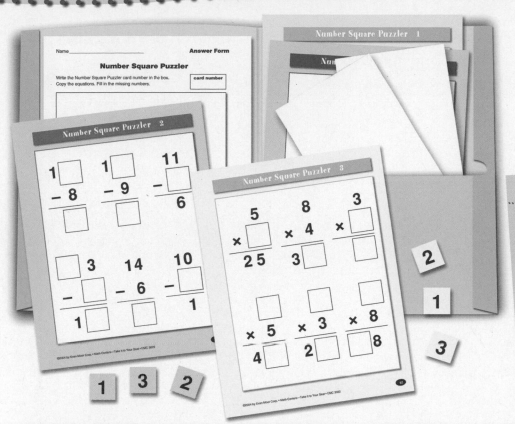

Preparing the Center

1. Prepare a folder following the directions on page 3.

   Cover—page 55
   Student Directions—page 57
   Number Squares—page 59
   Number Square Puzzler Cards—
       pages 61–67

2. Place each set of colored number squares in individual envelopes labeled 1 through 4. Place the envelopes in the right-hand pocket of the folder.

3. Reproduce a supply of the answer form on page 54. Place copies in the left-hand pocket of the folder.

Using the Center

1. The student selects a Number Square Puzzler card and writes its number in the box on the answer form. The student also takes the matching envelope of number squares.

2. Next, the student uses the number squares (0 through 9) to fill in the blank boxes in the equations. The student may use each number only once.

3. When all the missing numbers have been placed, the student copies the completed problems onto the answer form.

Answer Form

Number Square Puzzler

Write the Number Square Puzzler card number in the box.
Copy the equations. Fill in the missing numbers.

card number

Bonus: Make up a new set of puzzles. Use all of the numbers from 0 to 9.

Math Centers—Take It to Your Seat • EMC 3022 • ©2004 by Evan-Moor Corp.

Number Square Puzzler

Follow these steps:

1. Select a Number Square Puzzler card and write its number in the box on the answer form. Also take the matching envelope of number squares.

2. Use the number squares to fill in the blank boxes. Use each number square only one time.

3. Copy the completed problems onto the answer form.

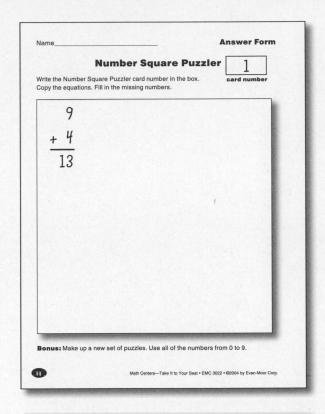

Name_____   Answer Form

Number Square Puzzler   `1`
card number

Write the Number Square Puzzler card number in the box.
Copy the equations. Fill in the missing numbers.

$$\begin{array}{r} 9 \\ + \ 4 \\ \hline 13 \end{array}$$

Bonus: Make up a new set of puzzles. Use all of the numbers from 0 to 9.

Math Centers—Take It to Your Seat • EMC 3022 • ©2004 by Evan-Moor Corp.

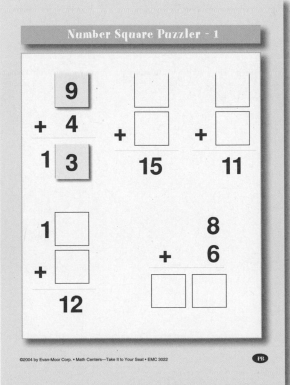

Number Square Puzzler - 1

©2004 by Evan-Moor Corp. • Math Centers—Take It to Your Seat • EMC 3022

Number Squares

0	1	2	3	4
5	6	7	8	9
0	1	2	3	4
5	6	7	8	9
0	1	2	3	4
5	6	7	8	9
0	1	2	3	4
5	6	7	8	9

1	1	1	1	1
1	1	1	1	1
2	2	2	2	2
2	2	2	2	2
3	3	3	3	3
3	3	3	3	3
4	4	4	4	4
4	4	4	4	4

Math Centers—Take It to Your Seat • EMC 3022 • ©2004 by Evan-Moor Corp.

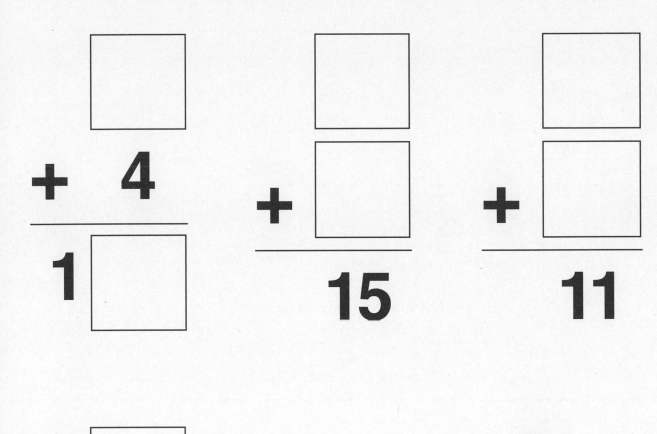

$$+ \quad 4$$
$$\overline{}$$
$$1 \quad \square$$

$$+ \quad \square$$
$$\overline{}$$
$$15$$

$$+ \quad \square$$
$$\overline{}$$
$$11$$

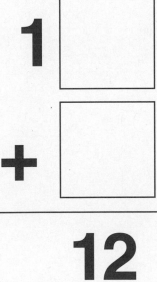

$$1 \quad \square$$
$$+ \quad \square$$
$$\overline{}$$
$$12$$

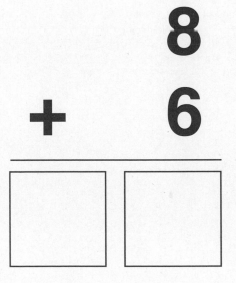

$$8$$
$$+ \quad 6$$
$$\overline{}$$
$$\square \quad \square$$

Number Square Puzzler 1

EMC 3022
©2004 by Evan-Moor Corp.

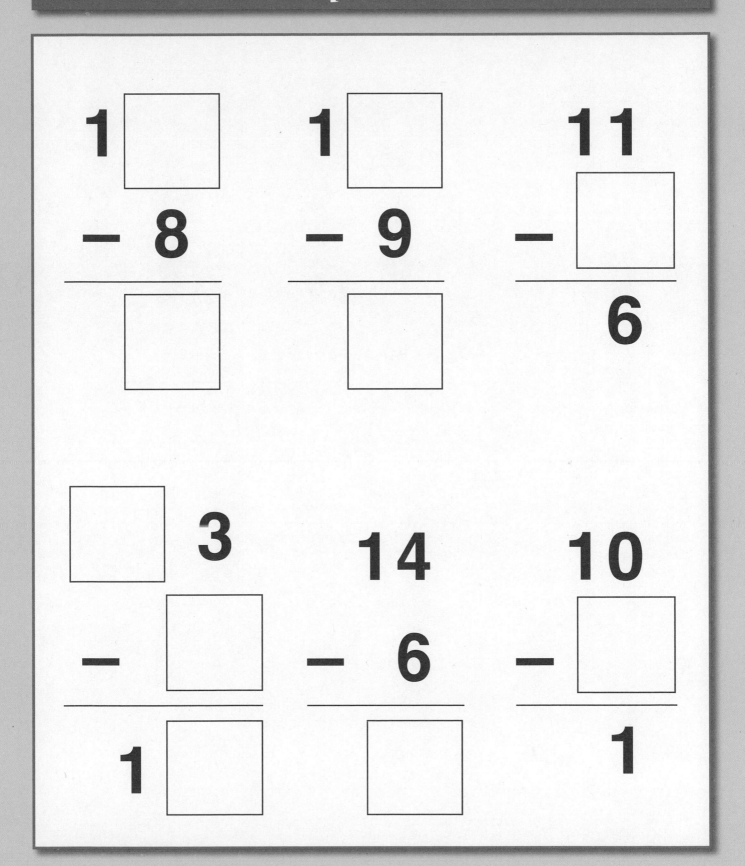

Number Square Puzzler 2

EMC 3022
©2004 by Evan-Moor Corp.

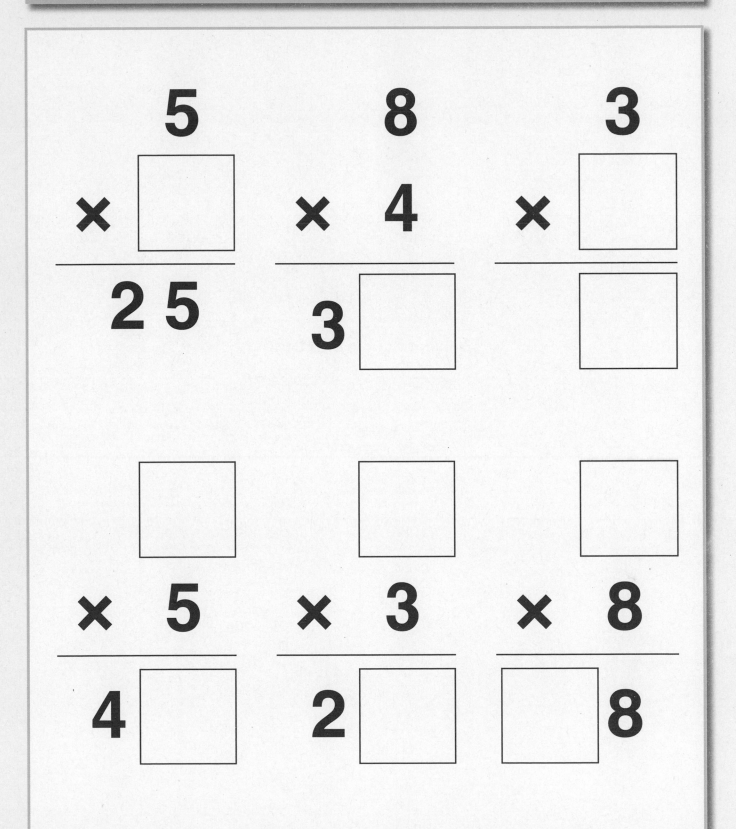

Number Square Puzzler 3

EMC 3022
©2004 by Evan-Moor Corp.

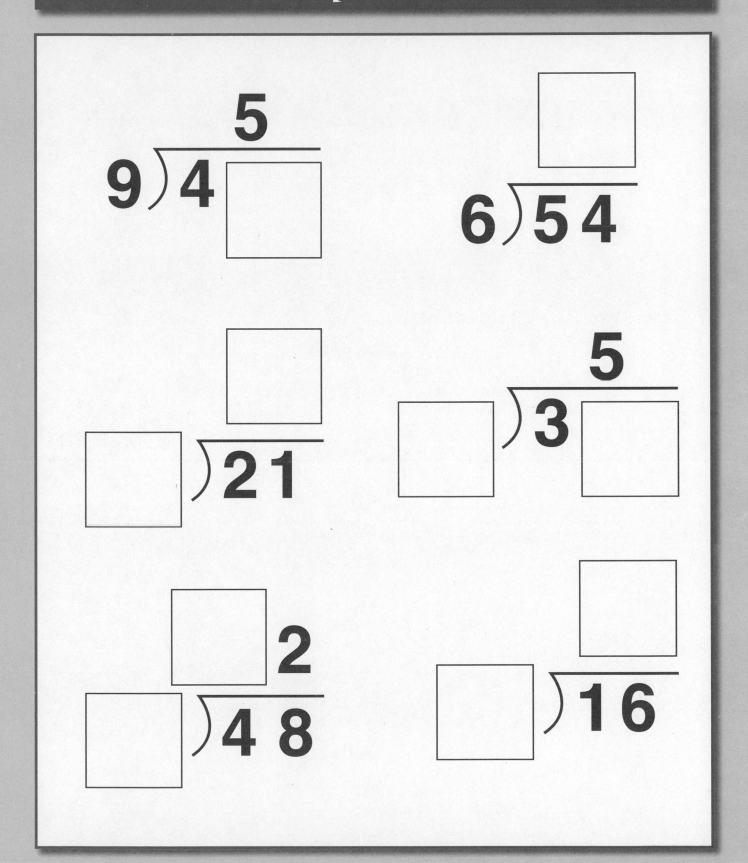

Number Square Puzzler 4

EMC 3022
©2004 by Evan-Moor Corp.

Read a Graph

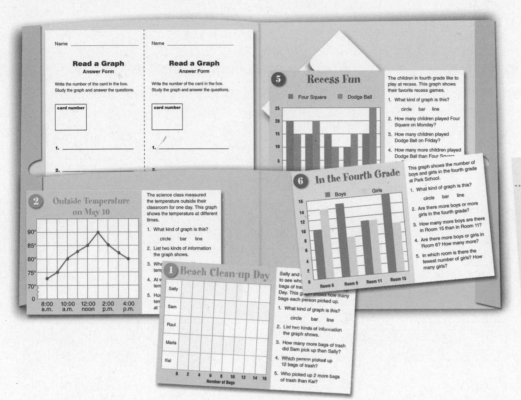

Preparing the Center

1. Prepare a folder following the directions on page 3.

   Cover—page 71
   Student Directions—page 73
   Task Cards—pages 75–79

2. Reproduce a supply of the answer form on page 70. Place copies in the left-hand pocket of the folder.

Using the Center

1. The student selects a task card and writes the card number on the answer form.

2. Next, the student studies the graph on the card.

3. Finally, the student answers questions relating to the graph.

4. If there is time, the student selects other cards and answers questions about those graphs.

Name _____

Read a Graph
Answer Form

Write the number of the card in the box.
Study the graph and answer the questions.

card number

1. _____

2. _____

3. _____

4. _____

5. _____

Bonus: On the back of this form, write two
more questions about the graph.
Write the answers to the questions.

Name _____

Read a Graph
Answer Form

Write the number of the card in the box.
Study the graph and answer the questions.

card number

1. _____

2. _____

3. _____

4. _____

5. _____

Bonus: On the back of this form, write two
more questions about the graph.
Write the answers to the questions.

Follow these steps:

1. Select a task card. Write the number of the card in the box on the answer form.

2. Study the graph and read the questions.

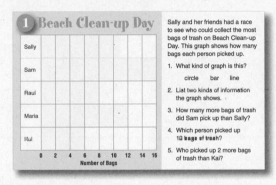

3. Write the answers on the answer form.

4. Select another card and repeat the steps.

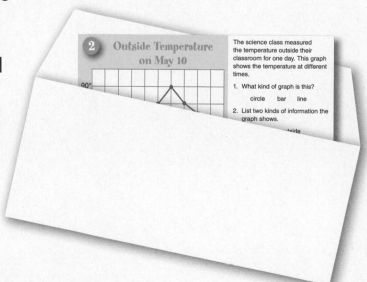

1 Beach Clean-up Day

Sally

Sam

Raul

Maria

Kai

0   2   4   6   8   10   12   14   16

Number of Bags

Sally and her friends had a race to see who could collect the most bags of trash on Beach Clean-up Day. This graph shows how many bags each person picked up.

1. What kind of graph is this?

   circle   bar   line

2. List two kinds of information the graph shows.

3. How many more bags of trash did Sam pick up than Sally?

4. Which person picked up 12 bags of trash?

5. Who picked up 2 more bags of trash than Kai?

2 Outside Temperature on May 10

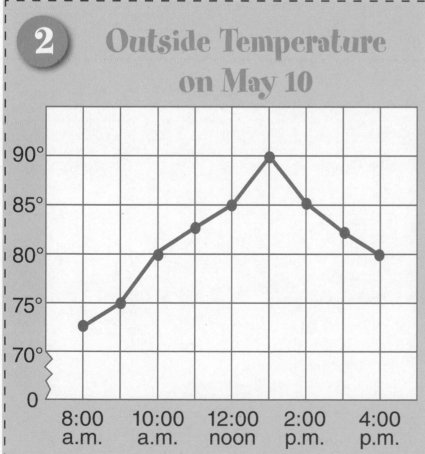

90°
85°
80°
75°
70°
0

8:00 a.m.   10:00 a.m.   12:00 noon   2:00 p.m.   4:00 p.m.

The science class measured the temperature outside their classroom for one day. This graph shows the temperature at different times.

1. What kind of graph is this?

   circle   bar   line

2. List two kinds of information the graph shows.

3. What was the outside temperature at 9:00 a.m.?

4. At what time was the hottest temperature? How hot was it?

5. How much cooler was the temperature at 4:00 than at 12:00?

Read a Graph

EMC 3022
©2004 by Evan-Moor Corp.

Read a Graph

EMC 3022
©2004 by Evan-Moor Corp.

③ Sweet Tooth

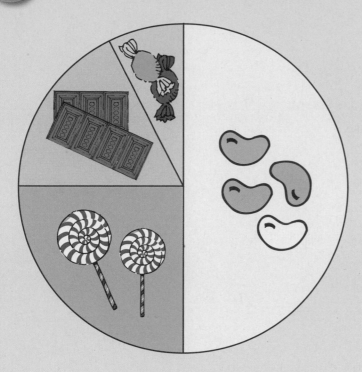

Max has a sweet tooth. He loves candy. He stopped at the candy store to buy a bag of candy. This graph shows the different kinds of candy in Max's bag.

1. What kind of graph is this?

    circle   bar   line

2. List two kinds of information the graph shows.

3. Can you tell from the graph which candy Max likes the best? Explain your answer.

4. Did Max buy more lollipops or jelly beans?

5. Did Max buy fewer hard candies or chocolate bars?

④ Pizza Party

Jerome had a pizza party for his birthday. This graph shows how many slices of pizza were eaten by Jerome and his guests.

1. What kind of graph is this?

    bar   circle   line

2. How many people ate exactly one slice of pizza?

3. How many slices of pizza were eaten at the party?

4. What is the largest number of slices of pizza eaten by one person?

5. What do the numbers along the side of the graph stand for?

Read a Graph

EMC 3022
©2004 by Evan-Moor Corp.

Read a Graph

EMC 3022
©2004 by Evan-Moor Corp.

5 Recess Fun

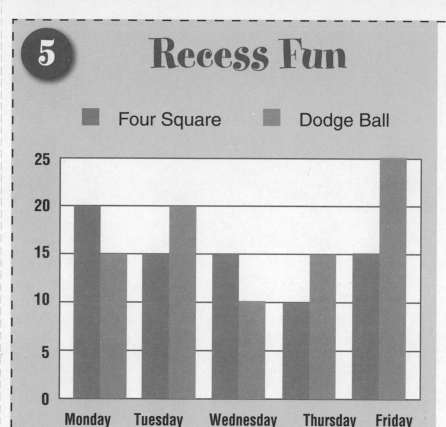

Four Square   **Dodge Ball**

The children in fourth grade like to play at recess. This graph shows their favorite recess games.

1. What kind of graph is this?

   circle   bar   line

2. How many children played Four Square on Monday?

3. How many children played Dodge Ball on Friday?

4. How many more children played Dodge Ball than Four Square on Friday?

5. What game did the most children play last week?

6 In the Fourth Grade

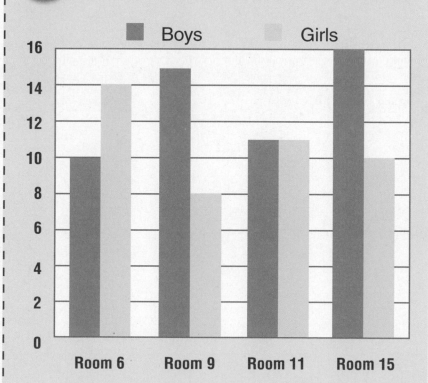

Boys   **Girls**

This graph shows the number of boys and girls in the fourth grade at Park School.

1. What kind of graph is this?

   circle   bar   line

2. Are there more boys or more girls in the fourth grade?

3. How many more boys are there in Room 15 than in Room 11?

4. Are there more boys or girls in Room 6? How many more?

5. In which room is there the fewest number of girls? How many girls?

Read a Graph

EMC 3022
©2004 by Evan-Moor Corp.

Read a Graph

EMC 3022
©2004 by Evan-Moor Corp.

Make a Graph

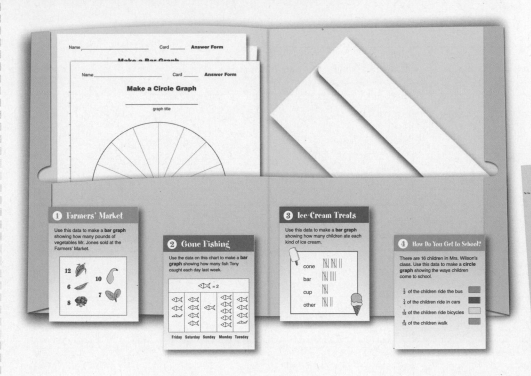

Preparing the Center

1. Prepare a folder following the directions on page 3.

   Cover—page 85
   Student Directions—page 87
   Task Cards—pages 89, 91

2. Reproduce a supply of the answer forms on pages 82–84. Place copies in the left-hand pocket of the folder.

Using the Center

1. The student selects a task card.

2. After reading the card, the student selects the correct graph answer form, writes the card number in the box on the form, and then creates a graph using the information on the card.

3. If there is time, the student selects another card and the appropriate graph answer form, and then creates a second graph.

Make a Bar Graph

_____

graph title

___					
___					
___					
___					
___					
___					
___					
___					
___					
___					

___ ___ ___ ___ ___

Bonus: On the back of this form, write three questions about the graph. Write the answers to the questions.

Make a Line Graph

_____

,   graph title

_____   _____   _____   _____   _____

Bonus: On the back of this form, write three questions about the graph. Write the answers to the questions.

Make a Circle Graph

_____

graph title

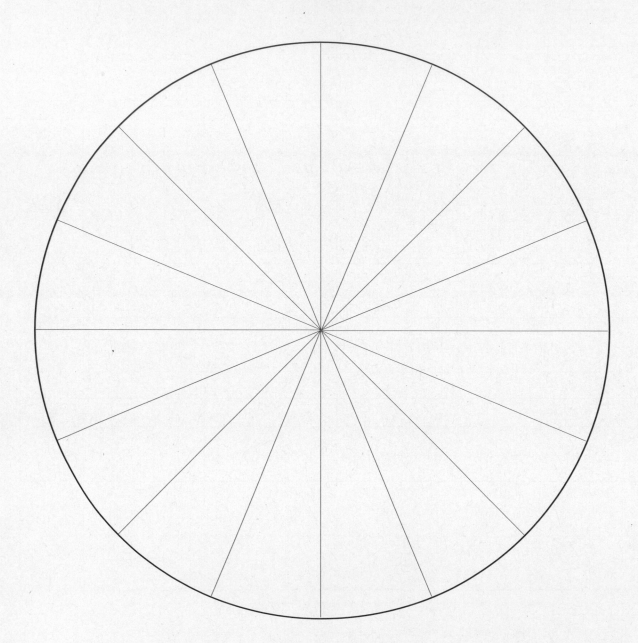

Bonus: On the back of this form, write three questions about the graph. Write the answers to the questions.

Make a Graph

= × 1 5 0 > ÷ 7 9 3 < 6 + = 2 4 8 × ÷

Make a Graph

Follow these steps:

1. Take a card and read it.

2. Pick the correct graph answer form and write the card number on the answer form.

3. Use the information on the card to make a graph.

4. If there is time, pick a new card and answer form and make a new graph.

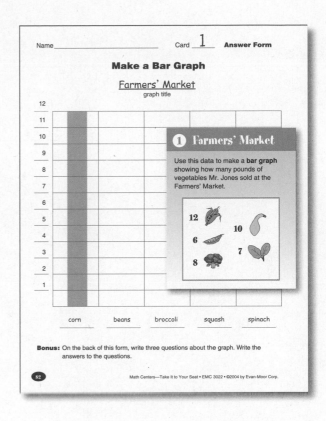

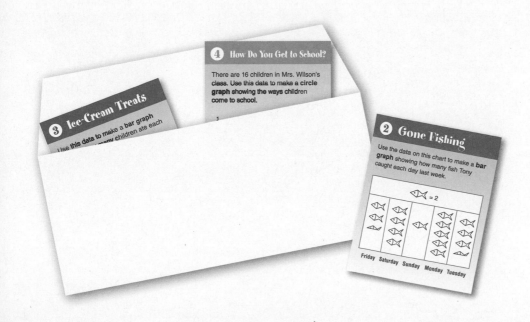

Math Centers—Take It to Your Seat • EMC 3022 • ©2004 by Evan-Moor Corp.

① Farmers' Market

Use this data to make a **bar graph** showing how many pounds of vegetables Mr. Jones sold at the Farmers' Market.

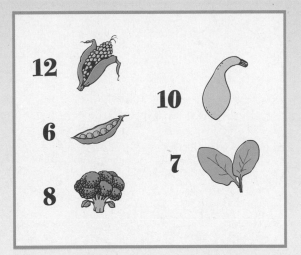

② Gone Fishing

Use the data on this chart to make a **bar graph** showing how many fish Tony caught each day last week.

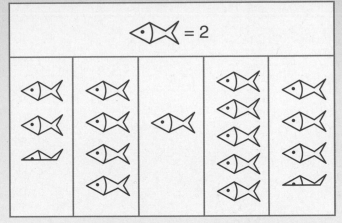

Friday   Saturday   Sunday   Monday   Tuesday

③ Ice-Cream Treats

Use this data to make a **bar graph** showing how many children ate each kind of ice cream.

cone

bar

cup

other

④ How Do You Get to School?

There are 16 children in Mrs. Wilson's class. Use this data to make a **circle graph** showing the ways children come to school.

$\frac{1}{2}$ of the children ride the bus

$\frac{1}{4}$ of the children ride in cars

$\frac{1}{16}$ of the children ride bicycles

$\frac{3}{16}$ of the children walk

Make a Graph

EMC 3022
©2004 by Evan-Moor Corp.

Make a Graph

EMC 3022
©2004 by Evan-Moor Corp.

Make a Graph

EMC 3022
©2004 by Evan-Moor Corp.

Make a Graph

EMC 3022
©2004 by Evan-Moor Corp.

5 What's the Temperature?

Ken checked the temperature outside his bedroom every day at noon. He wrote the temperature on a piece of paper.

Monday	60°
Tuesday	65°
Wednesday	70°
Thursday	60°
Friday	65°

Use this data to make a **line graph** to show how the temperature changed.

6 Bake Sale

The bake sale was a big success. Joyce listed the baked goods that were sold.

pies	3
cakes	6
cookies	4
doughnuts	1
muffins	2

Use this data to make a **circle graph** to show the sales.

7 Wonder World

A new theme park named Wonder World opened in June. This many people visited the park in the first five months.

June	9,000
July	12,000
August	11,000
September	7,000
October	5,000

Use this data to make a **bar graph** to show the number of people that visited the park during that time period.

8 Super Shoe Sale

The store manager made a chart to follow the sales of his clerks during the week of a back-to-school sale.

Monday—George (6 sales), Marge (5 sales)
Tuesday—George (4 sales), Marge (7 sales)
Wednesday—George (2 sales), Marge (3 sales)
Thursday—George (5 sales), Marge (5 sales)
Friday—George (10 sales), Marge (8 sales)

Use this data to make a **line graph** to show how both clerks' sales went up during the sale. Use blue to show George's sales. Use red to show Marge's sales.

Make a Graph

EMC 3022
©2004 by Evan-Moor Corp.

Make a Graph

EMC 3022
©2004 by Evan-Moor Corp.

Make a Graph

EMC 3022
©2004 by Evan-Moor Corp.

Make a Graph

EMC 3022
©2004 by Evan-Moor Corp.

How Many Combinations?

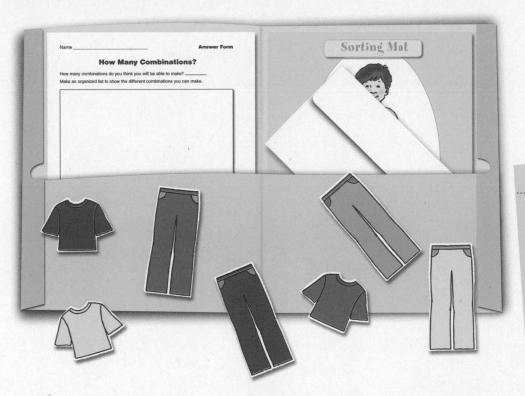

Preparing the Center

1. Prepare a folder following the directions on page 3.

   Cover—page 95
   Student Directions—page 97
   Clothing Cutouts—page 99
   Sorting Mat—page 101

2. Reproduce a supply of the answer form on page 94. Place copies in the left-hand pocket of the folder.

Using the Center

1. The student takes the envelope of clothing cutouts, the sorting mat, and an answer form.

2. Next, the student places shirts and pants on the boy on the sorting mat in various combinations.

3. The student creates an organized list of the different combinations made.

How Many Combinations?

How many combinations do you think you will be able to make? _____

Make an organized list to show the different combinations you can make.

Bonus: How many combinations could you make if you added a yellow shirt and a pair of green pants?

How Many Combinations?

Follow these steps:

1. Take the envelope of clothing cutouts, the sorting mat, and an answer form.

2. Think about how many combinations you will be able to make. Write your estimate on the answer form.

3. Lay a shirt and pants on the boy on the sorting mat. List the color combination on the answer form.

4. Continue making and listing the combinations of shirts and pants. See how many combinations you can make in all.

Name_____   Answer Form

How Many Combinations?

How many combinations do you think you will be able to make? _____
Make an organized list to show the different combinations you can make.

Bonus: How many combinations could you make if you added a yellow shirt and a pair of green pants?

91

©2004 by Evan-Moor Corp. • Math Centers—Take It to Your Seat • EMC 3022

Sorting Mat

101

Math Centers—Take It to Your Seat • EMC 3022 • ©2004 by Evan-Moor Corp.

How Many Combinations?

How Many Combinations?

How Many Combinations?

How Many Combinations?

How Many Combinations?

How Many Combinations?

How Many Combinations?

Sorting Mat

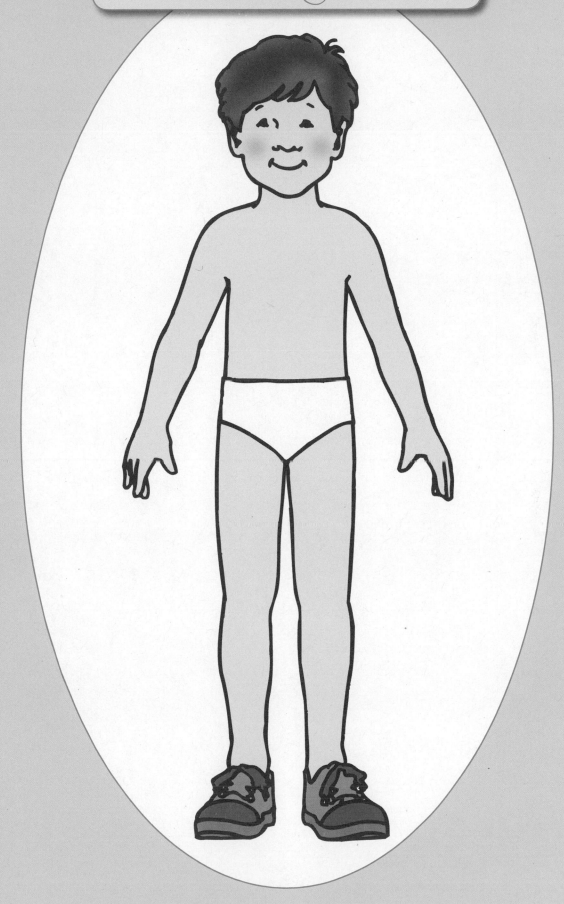

How Many Combinations?

EMC 3022

©2004 by Evan-Moor Corp.

Name That Part!

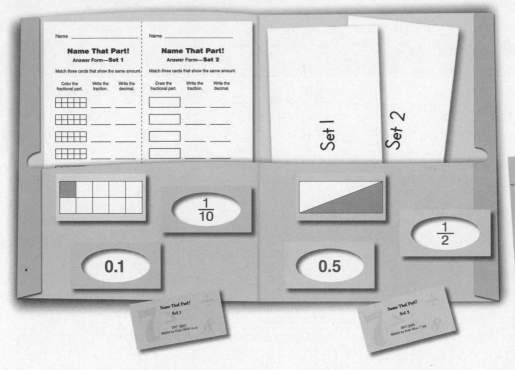

Preparing the Center

1. Prepare a folder following the directions on page 3.

   Cover—page 105
   Student Directions—page 107
   Task Cards—pages 109–119

2. Reproduce a supply of the answer forms on page 104. Place copies in the left-hand pocket of the folder.

Using the Center

1. The student selects a set of task cards and the matching answer form.

2. Next, the student matches three cards that show the same amount.

3. The student either colors (Set 1) or draws (Set 2) the fractional part, and then writes the fraction and decimal amounts on the answer form.

Name _____

Name That Part!

Answer Form—Set 1

Match three cards that show the same amount.

Color the fractional part.	Write the fraction.	Write the decimal.

Name _____

Name That Part!

Answer Form—Set 2

Match three cards that show the same amount.

Draw the fractional part.	Write the fraction.	Write the decimal.

Math Centers—Take It to Your Seat • EMC 3022 • ©2004 by Evan-Moor Corp.

Name That Part!

Follow these steps:

Set 1

1. Select the Set 1 cards and a Set 1 answer form.

2. Match three cards that show the same amount.

3. Color the fractional part.
   Write the fraction.
   Write the decimal.

4. Continue matching cards, repeating Steps 2 and 3.

Set 2

1. Select the Set 2 cards and a Set 2 answer form.

2. Match three cards that show the same amount.

3. Draw the fractional part.
   Write the fraction.
   Write the decimal.

4. Continue matching cards, repeating Steps 2 and 3.

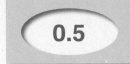

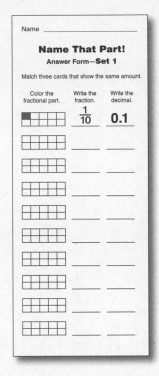

= × ÷

1 5 <

0

7 3 ÷

< 9

7 6 +

= 2 4

8 × ÷

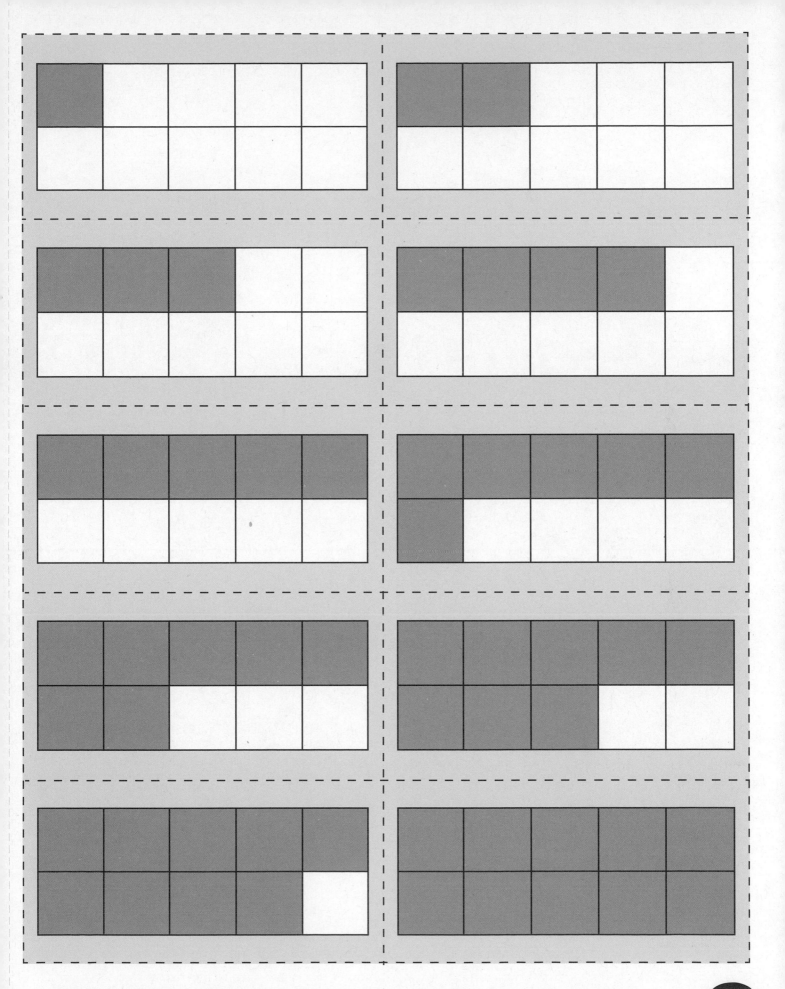

Name That Part!

Set 1

EMC 3022
©2004 by Evan-Moor Corp.

Name That Part!

Set 1

EMC 3022
©2004 by Evan-Moor Corp.

Name That Part!

Set 1

EMC 3022
©2004 by Evan-Moor Corp.

Name That Part!

Set 1

EMC 3022
©2004 by Evan-Moor Corp.

Name That Part!

Set 1

EMC 3022
©2004 by Evan-Moor Corp.

Name That Part!

Set 1

EMC 3022
©2004 by Evan-Moor Corp.

Name That Part!

Set 1

EMC 3022
©2004 by Evan-Moor Corp.

Name That Part!

Set 1

EMC 3022
©2004 by Evan-Moor Corp.

$\dfrac{1}{10}$

$\dfrac{2}{10}$

$\dfrac{3}{10}$

$\dfrac{4}{10}$

$\dfrac{5}{10}$

$\dfrac{6}{10}$

$\dfrac{7}{10}$

$\dfrac{8}{10}$

$\dfrac{9}{10}$

$\dfrac{10}{10}$ or 1

Name That Part!

Set 1

EMC 3022
©2004 by Evan-Moor Corp.

Name That Part!

Set 1

EMC 3022
©2004 by Evan-Moor Corp.

Name That Part!

Set 1

EMC 3022
©2004 by Evan-Moor Corp.

Name That Part!

Set 1

EMC 3022
©2004 by Evan-Moor Corp.

Name That Part!

Set 1

EMC 3022
©2004 by Evan-Moor Corp.

Name That Part!

Set 1

EMC 3022
©2004 by Evan-Moor Corp.

Name That Part!

Set 1

EMC 3022
©2004 by Evan-Moor Corp.

Name That Part!

Set 1

EMC 3022
©2004 by Evan-Moor Corp.

Name That Part!

Set 1

EMC 3022
©2004 by Evan-Moor Corp.

Name That Part!

Set 1

EMC 3022
©2004 by Evan-Moor Corp.

0.1

0.2

0.3

0.4

0.5

0.6

0.7

0.8

0.9

1.0

Name That Part!

Set 1

EMC 3022
©2004 by Evan-Moor Corp.

Name That Part!

Set 1

EMC 3022
©2004 by Evan-Moor Corp.

Name That Part!

Set 1

EMC 3022
©2004 by Evan-Moor Corp.

Name That Part!

Set 1

EMC 3022
©2004 by Evan-Moor Corp.

Name That Part!

Set 1

EMC 3022
©2004 by Evan-Moor Corp.

Name That Part!

Set 1

EMC 3022
©2004 by Evan-Moor Corp.

Name That Part!

Set 1

EMC 3022
©2004 by Evan-Moor Corp.

Name That Part!

Set 1

EMC 3022
©2004 by Evan-Moor Corp.

Name That Part!

Set 1

EMC 3022
©2004 by Evan-Moor Corp.

Name That Part!

Set 1

EMC 3022
©2004 by Evan-Moor Corp.

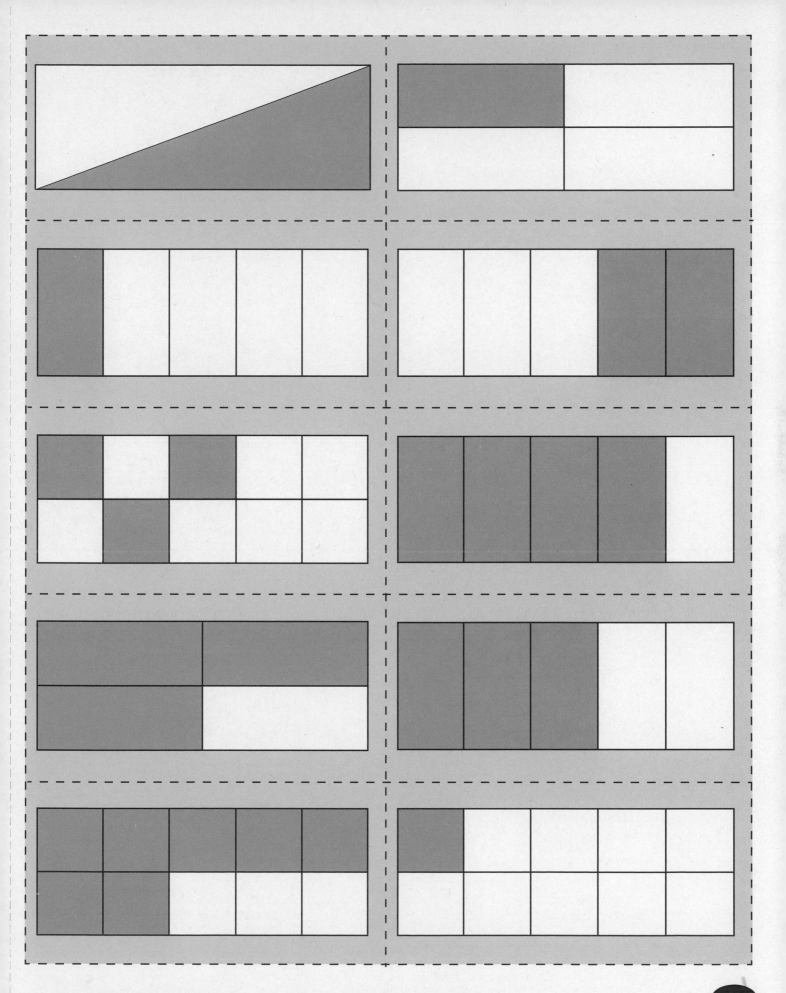

Name That Part!

Set 2

EMC 3022
©2004 by Evan-Moor Corp.

Name That Part!

Set 2

EMC 3022
©2004 by Evan-Moor Corp.

Name That Part!

Set 2

EMC 3022
©2004 by Evan-Moor Corp.

Name That Part!

Set 2

EMC 3022
©2004 by Evan-Moor Corp.

Name That Part!

Set 2

EMC 3022
©2004 by Evan-Moor Corp.

Name That Part!

Set 2

EMC 3022
©2004 by Evan-Moor Corp.

Name That Part!

Set 2

EMC 3022
©2004 by Evan-Moor Corp.

Name That Part!

Set 2

EMC 3022
©2004 by Evan-Moor Corp.

Name That Part!

Set 2

EMC 3022
©2004 by Evan-Moor Corp.

Name That Part!

Set 2

EMC 3022
©2004 by Evan-Moor Corp.

$\dfrac{1}{2}$

$\dfrac{1}{4}$

$\dfrac{1}{5}$

$\dfrac{2}{5}$

$\dfrac{3}{10}$

$\dfrac{4}{5}$

$\dfrac{3}{4}$

$\dfrac{3}{5}$

$\dfrac{7}{10}$

$\dfrac{1}{10}$

Name That Part!

Set 2

EMC 3022
©2004 by Evan-Moor Corp.

Name That Part!

Set 2

EMC 3022
©2004 by Evan-Moor Corp.

Name That Part!

Set 2

EMC 3022
©2004 by Evan-Moor Corp.

Name That Part!

Set 2

EMC 3022
©2004 by Evan-Moor Corp.

Name That Part!

Set 2

EMC 3022
©2004 by Evan-Moor Corp.

Name That Part!

Set 2

EMC 3022
©2004 by Evan-Moor Corp.

Name That Part!

Set 2

EMC 3022
©2004 by Evan-Moor Corp.

Name That Part!

Set 2

EMC 3022
©2004 by Evan-Moor Corp.

Name That Part!

Set 2

EMC 3022
©2004 by Evan-Moor Corp.

Name That Part!

Set 2

EMC 3022
©2004 by Evan-Moor Corp.

0.7	0.1
0.4	0.6
0.8	0.5
0.3	0.75
0.25	0.2

Name That Part!

Set 2

EMC 3022
©2004 by Evan-Moor Corp.

Name That Part!

Set 2

EMC 3022
©2004 by Evan-Moor Corp.

Name That Part!

Set 2

EMC 3022
©2004 by Evan-Moor Corp.

Name That Part!

Set 2

EMC 3022
©2004 by Evan-Moor Corp.

Name That Part!

Set 2

EMC 3022
©2004 by Evan-Moor Corp.

Name That Part!

Set 2

EMC 3022
©2004 by Evan-Moor Corp.

Name That Part!

Set 2

EMC 3022
©2004 by Evan-Moor Corp.

Name That Part!

Set 2

EMC 3022
©2004 by Evan-Moor Corp.

Name That Part!

Set 2

EMC 3022
©2004 by Evan-Moor Corp.

Name That Part!

Set 2

EMC 3022
©2004 by Evan-Moor Corp.

Plotting a Picture

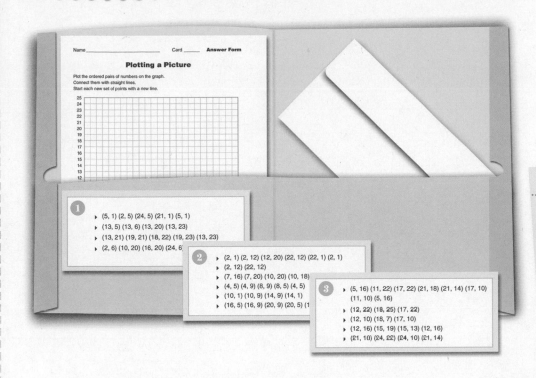

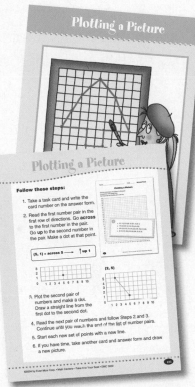

Preparing the Center

1. Prepare a folder following the directions on page 3.

   Cover—page 123
   Student Directions—page 125
   Task Cards—pages 127, 129

2. Reproduce a supply of the answer form on page 122. Place copies in the left-hand pocket of the folder.

Using the Center

1. The student selects a task card and writes the card number on the answer form.

2. Next, the student plots the ordered pairs of numbers on the graph in the order in which they are listed, connecting them with straight lines.

3. The student may select another task card if time allows.

Plotting a Picture

Plot the ordered pairs of numbers on the graph.

Connect them with straight lines.

Start each new set of points with a new line.

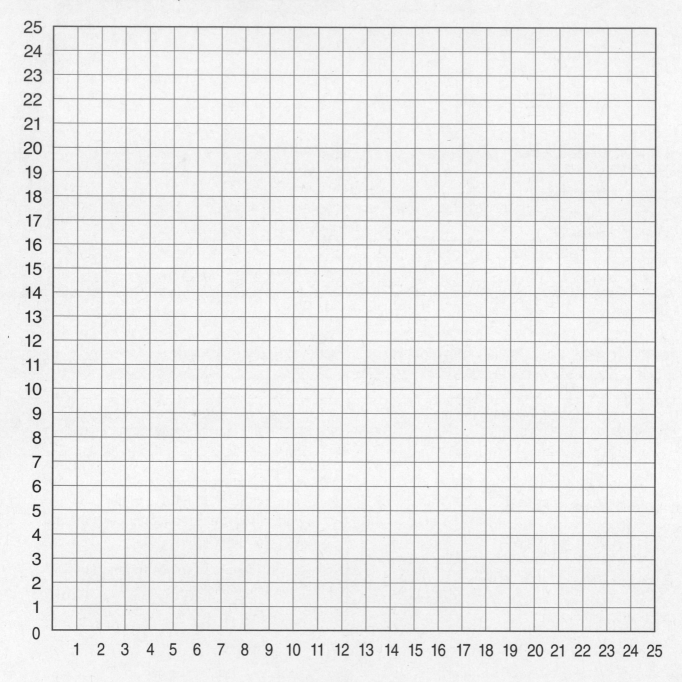

Plotting a Picture

Follow these steps:

1. Take a task card and write the card number on the answer form.

2. Read the first number pair in the first row of directions. Go **across** to the first number in the pair. Go **up** to the second number in the pair. Make a dot at that point.

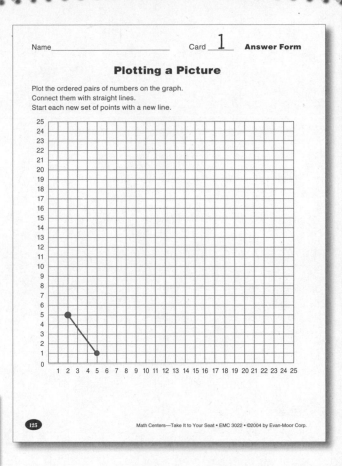

1
- (5, 1) (2, 5) (24, 5) (21, 1) (5, 1)
- (13, 5) (13, 6) (13, 20) (13, 23)
- (13, 21) (19, 21) (18, 22) (19, 23) (13, 23)
- (2, 6) (10, 20) (16, 20) (24, 6) (2, 6)

3. Plot the second pair of numbers and make a dot. Draw a straight line from the first dot to the second dot.

(5, 1) = ⟶ **across 5**
↑ **up 1**

(2, 5) = ⟶ **across 2**
↑ **up 5**

4. Read the next pair of numbers and follow Steps 2 and 3. Continue until you reach the end of the list of number pairs.

5. Start each new set of points with a new line.

6. If you have time, take another card and answer form and draw a new picture.

1

▶ (5, 1) (2, 5) (24, 5) (21, 1) (5, 1)

▶ (13, 5) (13, 6) (13, 20) (13, 23)

▶ (13, 21) (19, 21) (18, 22) (19, 23) (13, 23)

▶ (2, 6) (10, 20) (16, 20) (24, 6) (2, 6)

2

▶ (2, 1) (2, 12) (12, 20) (22, 12) (22, 1) (2, 1)

▶ (2, 12) (22, 12)

▶ (7, 16) (7, 20) (10, 20) (10, 18)

▶ (4, 5) (4, 9) (8, 9) (8, 5) (4, 5)

▶ (10, 1) (10, 9) (14, 9) (14, 1)

▶ (16, 5) (16, 9) (20, 9) (20, 5) (16, 5)

3

▶ (5, 16) (11, 22) (17, 22) (21, 18) (21, 14) (17, 10) (11, 10) (5, 16)

▶ (12, 22) (18, 25) (17, 22)

▶ (12, 10) (18, 7) (17, 10)

▶ (12, 16) (15, 19) (15, 13) (12, 16)

▶ (21, 18) (24, 22) (24, 10) (21, 14)

Plotting a Picture

EMC 3022
©2004 by Evan-Moor Corp.

Plotting a Picture

EMC 3022
©2004 by Evan-Moor Corp.

Plotting a Picture

EMC 3022
©2004 by Evan-Moor Corp.

4

▶ (19, 0) (10, 10) (7, 10) (1, 15) (1, 21) (4, 24) (10, 24) (15, 19) (15, 15) (25, 6) (19, 6) (19, 0)

▶ (4, 15) (6, 18) (4, 21) (8, 20) (11, 22) (11, 18) (14, 16) (10, 16) (10, 12) (8, 15) (4, 15)

▶ (14, 9) (14, 11) (18, 7)

▶ (17, 6) (19, 8)

5

▶ (11, 0) (11, 6) (8, 6) (4, 9) (4, 14) (3, 14) (2, 13) (1, 13) (1, 18) (2, 18) (3, 17) (4, 17) (5, 19) (7, 25) (19, 25) (21, 19) (22, 17) (23, 17) (24, 18) (25, 18) (25, 13) (24, 13) (23, 14) (22, 14) (22, 9) (18, 6) (15, 6) (15, 0)

▶ (7, 13) (9, 8) (17, 8) (19, 13) (17, 13) (15, 11) (11, 11) (9, 13) (7, 13)

▶ (8, 20) (10, 22) (11, 21) (9, 19) (8, 20)

▶ (15, 21) (16, 22) (18, 20) (17, 19) (15, 21)

▶ (12, 19) (12, 14) (14, 14) (15, 15)

6

▶ (7, 9) (7, 15) (14, 15) (14, 9) (7, 9)

▶ (9, 15) (9, 16) (8, 16) (8, 17) (7, 17) (7, 18) (8, 18) (8, 20) (12, 20) (12, 18) (13, 18) (13, 17) (12, 17) (12, 16) (11, 16) (11, 15)

▶ (7, 15) (4, 12) (4, 10) (6, 8) (6, 10) (5, 11) (7, 13)

▶ (14, 15) (17, 12) (17, 10) (15, 8) (15, 10) (16, 11) (14, 13)

▶ (8, 9) (8, 3) (7, 3) (7, 2) (10, 2) (10, 9)

▶ (11, 9) (11, 2) (14, 2) (14, 3) (13, 3) (13, 9)

▶ (9, 17) (11, 17)

▶ (9, 18) (10, 19) (11, 18) (9, 18)

▶ (10, 18) (10, 19)

Plotting a Picture

EMC 3022
©2004 by Evan-Moor Corp.

Plotting a Picture

EMC 3022
©2004 by Evan-Moor Corp.

Plotting a Picture

EMC 3022
©2004 by Evan-Moor Corp.

What's My Rule?

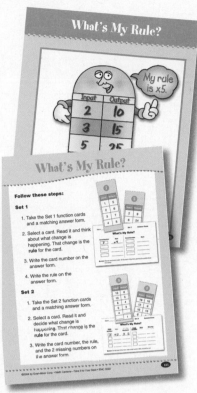

Preparing the Center

1. Prepare a folder following the directions on page 3.

   Cover—page 133
   Student Directions—page 135
   Function Cards—pages 137, 139

2. Reproduce a supply of the answer forms on page 132. Place copies in the left-hand pocket of the folder.

Using the Center

1. The student selects a set of function cards and the matching answer form.

2. Next, the student reads a card, writes its number in the box on the answer form, and determines the change that is occurring.

3. Finally, the student writes the rule. For Set 2, the student also writes the two missing numbers.

What's My Rule?

Card Number	Rule	Card Number	Rule
	_____		_____
	_____		_____
	_____		_____
	_____		_____

Bonus: Choose one function table. On the back of this form, continue the pattern three more times.

- -

Name_____ Set 2   Answer Form

What's My Rule?

Card Number	Rule	Missing Numbers	Card Number	Rule	Missing Numbers
	_____	___ , ___		_____	___ , ___
	_____	___ , ___		_____	___ , ___
	_____	___ , ___		_____	___ , ___
	_____	___ , ___		_____	___ , ___

Bonus: On the back of this form, write a new function table and tell the rule.

Follow these steps:

Set 1

1. Take the Set 1 function cards and a matching answer form.

2. Select a card. Read it and think about what change is happening. That change is the **rule** for the card.

3. Write the card number on the answer form.

4. Write the rule on the answer form.

Set 2

1. Take the Set 2 function cards and a matching answer form.

2. Select a card. Read it and decide what change is happening. That change is the **rule** for the card.

3. Write the card number, the rule, and the 2 missing numbers on the answer form.

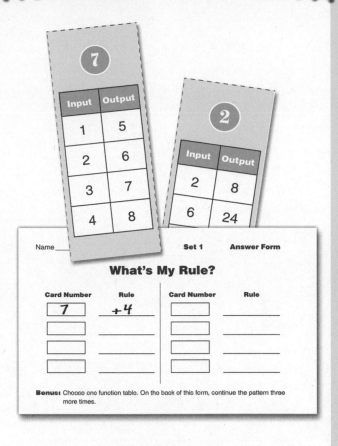

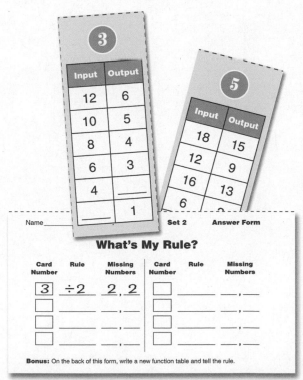

1

Input	Output
1	3
6	8
3	5
4	6

2

Input	Output
2	8
6	24
4	16
7	28

3

Input	Output
9	4
16	11
14	9
8	3

4

Input	Output
12	6
24	12
18	9
4	2

5

Input	Output
4	2
8	6
5	3
9	7

6

Input	Output
9	3
3	1
24	8
18	6

7

Input	Output
1	5
2	6
3	7
4	8

8

Input	Output
1	5
3	15
6	30
8	40

What's My Rule?

Set 1

What's My Rule?

Set 1

What's My Rule?

Set 1

What's My Rule?

Set 1

What's My Rule?

Set 1

What's My Rule?

Set 1

What's My Rule?

Set 1

What's My Rule?

Set 1

1

Input	Output
1	2
2	4
3	6
4	8
5	___
___	12

2

Input	Output
10	5
22	17
16	11
19	14
8	___
___	23

3

Input	Output
12	6
10	5
8	4
6	3
4	___
___	1

4

Input	Output
6	18
3	9
0	0
5	15
2	___
___	21

5

Input	Output
18	15
12	9
16	13
6	3
9	___
___	0

6

Input	Output
2	5
6	9
7	10
12	15
14	___
___	13

7

Input	Output
12	3
20	5
40	10
16	4
24	___
___	15

8

Input	Output
19	24
8	13
12	17
54	59
90	___
___	21

What's My Rule?

Set 2

What's My Rule?

Set 2

What's My Rule?

Set 2

What's My Rule?

Set 2

What's My Rule?

Set 2

What's My Rule?

Set 2

What's My Rule?

Set 2

What's My Rule?

Set 2

Analyze the Data

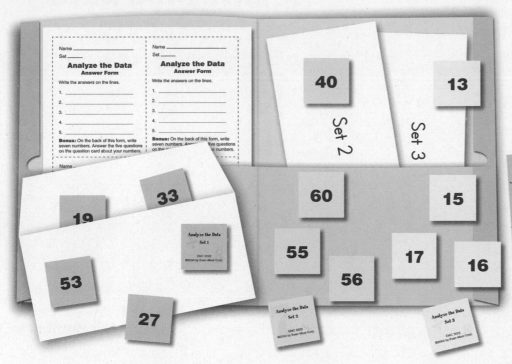

Preparing the Center

1. Prepare a folder following the directions on page 3.

   Cover—page 143
   Student Directions—page 145
   Number Cards—pages 147, 149
   Question Card—page 151

2. Reproduce a supply of the answer form on page 142. Place copies in the left-hand pocket of the folder.

Using the Center

1. The student takes the question card and selects a set of number cards. The student writes the set number on the answer form.

2. Next, the student arranges the number cards in order from smallest to largest. Using the numbers, the student answers the questions on the question card.

3. The student then writes the answer to each question on the answer form.

Name _____

Set _____

Analyze the Data
Answer Form

Write the answers on the lines.

1. _____

2. _____

3. _____

4. _____

5. _____

Bonus: On the back of this form, write
seven numbers. Answer the five questions
on the question card about your numbers.

Name _____

Set _____

Analyze the Data
Answer Form

Write the answers on the lines.

1. _____

2. _____

3. _____

4. _____

5. _____

Bonus: On the back of this form, write
seven numbers. Answer the five questions
on the question card about your numbers.

Name _____

Set _____

Analyze the Data
Answer Form

Write the answers on the lines.

1. _____

2. _____

3. _____

4. _____

5. _____

Bonus: On the back of this form, write
seven numbers. Answer the five questions
on the question card about your numbers.

Name _____

Set _____

Analyze the Data
Answer Form

Write the answers on the lines.

1. _____

2. _____

3. _____

4. _____

5. _____

Bonus: On the back of this form, write
seven numbers. Answer the five questions
on the question card about your numbers.

Math Centers—Take It to Your Seat • EMC 3022 • ©2004 by Evan-Moor Corp.

Follow these steps:

1. Choose a set of number cards and write the set number on the answer form.

2. Arrange the numbers in order from the smallest to the largest.

3. Take the question card.

4. Read and answer each question. Write the answers on the answer form.

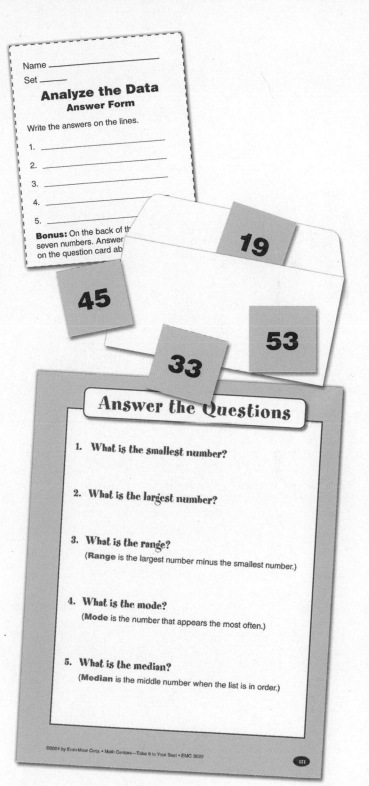

Name _____
Set _____

Analyze the Data
Answer Form

Write the answers on the lines.

1. _____
2. _____
3. _____
4. _____
5. _____

Bonus: On the back of th...
seven numbers. Answer...
on the question card ab...

Answer the Questions

1. **What is the smallest number?**

2. **What is the largest number?**

3. **What is the range?**
   (**Range** is the largest number minus the smallest number.)

4. **What is the mode?**
   (**Mode** is the number that appears the most often.)

5. **What is the median?**
   (**Median** is the middle number when the list is in order.)

©2004 by Evan-Moor Corp. • Math Centers—Take It to Your Seat • EMC 3022

151

= × 1 5 > 0 ÷ 7 9 3 > 6 + = 2 4 8 × ÷

19	33	53	27
33	18	45	
40	56	55	49
60	56	42	

Analyze the Data
Set 1

EMC 3022
©2004 by Evan-Moor Corp.

Analyze the Data
Set 1

EMC 3022
©2004 by Evan-Moor Corp.

Analyze the Data
Set 1

EMC 3022
©2004 by Evan-Moor Corp.

Analyze the Data
Set 1

EMC 3022
©2004 by Evan-Moor Corp.

Analyze the Data
Set 1

EMC 3022
©2004 by Evan-Moor Corp.

Analyze the Data
Set 1

EMC 3022
©2004 by Evan-Moor Corp.

Analyze the Data
Set 1

EMC 3022
©2004 by Evan-Moor Corp.

Analyze the Data
Set 2

EMC 3022
©2004 by Evan-Moor Corp.

Analyze the Data
Set 2

EMC 3022
©2004 by Evan-Moor Corp.

Analyze the Data
Set 2

EMC 3022
©2004 by Evan-Moor Corp.

Analyze the Data
Set 2

EMC 3022
©2004 by Evan-Moor Corp.

Analyze the Data
Set 2

EMC 3022
©2004 by Evan-Moor Corp.

Analyze the Data
Set 2

EMC 3022
©2004 by Evan-Moor Corp.

Analyze the Data
Set 2

EMC 3022
©2004 by Evan-Moor Corp.

13	**15**	**16**	**16**
17	**18**	**18**	**18**
19	**19**	**21**	**24**
25	**29**	**12**	

Analyze the Data
Set 3

Analyze the Data
Set 3

Analyze the Data
Set 3

Analyze the Data
Set 3

Analyze the Data
Set 3

Analyze the Data
Set 3

Analyze the Data
Set 3

Analyze the Data
Set 3

Analyze the Data
Set 3

Analyze the Data
Set 3

Analyze the Data
Set 3

Analyze the Data
Set 3

Analyze the Data
Set 3

Analyze the Data
Set 3

Analyze the Data
Set 3

1. **What is the smallest number?**

2. **What is the largest number?**

3. **What is the range?**

    (**Range** is the largest number minus the smallest number.)

4. **What is the mode?**

    (**Mode** is the number that appears the most often.)

5. **What is the median?**

    (**Median** is the middle number when the list is in order.)

Analyze the Data

EMC 3022
©2004 by Evan-Moor Corp.

Perimeter and Area

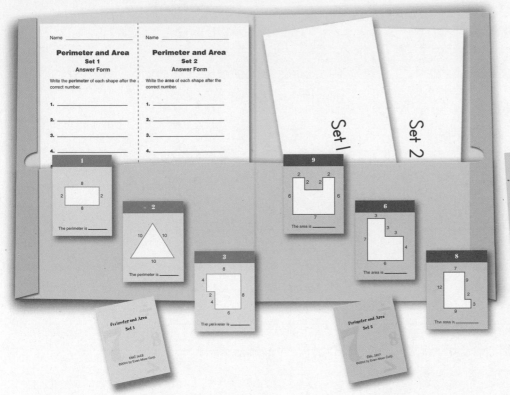

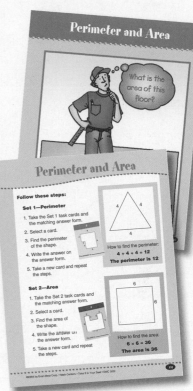

Preparing the Center

1. Prepare a folder following the directions on page 3.

   Cover—page 155
   Student Directions—page 157
   Task Cards—pages 159, 161

2. Reproduce a supply of the answer forms on page 154. Place copies in the left-hand pocket of the folder.

Using the Center

1. The student selects a set of task cards and the matching answer form.

2. For Set 1, the student finds the perimeter of each shape and writes the answers on the answer form.

3. For Set 2, the student finds the area of each shape and writes the answers on the answer form.

Name _____

Perimeter and Area
Set 1
Answer Form

Write the **perimeter** of each shape after the correct number.

1. _____

2. _____

3. _____

4. _____

5. _____

6. _____

7. _____

8. _____

9. _____

Bonus: On the back of this form, draw a shape with straight lines. Write a number on each side to tell how long it is. Then write the **perimeter** of your shape.

Name _____

Perimeter and Area
Set 2
Answer Form

Write the **area** of each shape after the correct number.

1. _____

2. _____

3. _____

4. _____

5. _____

6. _____

7. _____

8. _____

9. _____

Bonus: On the back of this form, draw a shape with straight lines. Write a number on each side to tell how long it is. Then write the **area** of your shape.

Perimeter and Area

Perimeter and Area

Follow these steps:

Set 1—Perimeter

1. Take the Set 1 task cards and the matching answer form.

2. Select a card.

3. Find the perimeter of the shape.

4. Write the answer on the answer form.

5. Take a new card and repeat the steps.

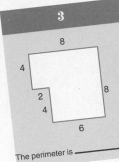

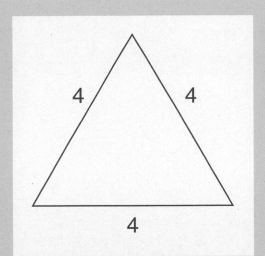

How to find the perimeter:

4 + 4 + 4 = 12

The perimeter is 12

Set 2—Area

1. Take the Set 2 task cards and the matching answer form.

2. Select a card.

3. Find the area of the shape.

4. Write the answer on the answer form.

5. Take a new card and repeat the steps.

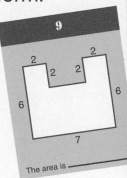

How to find the area:

6 × 6 = 36

The area is 36

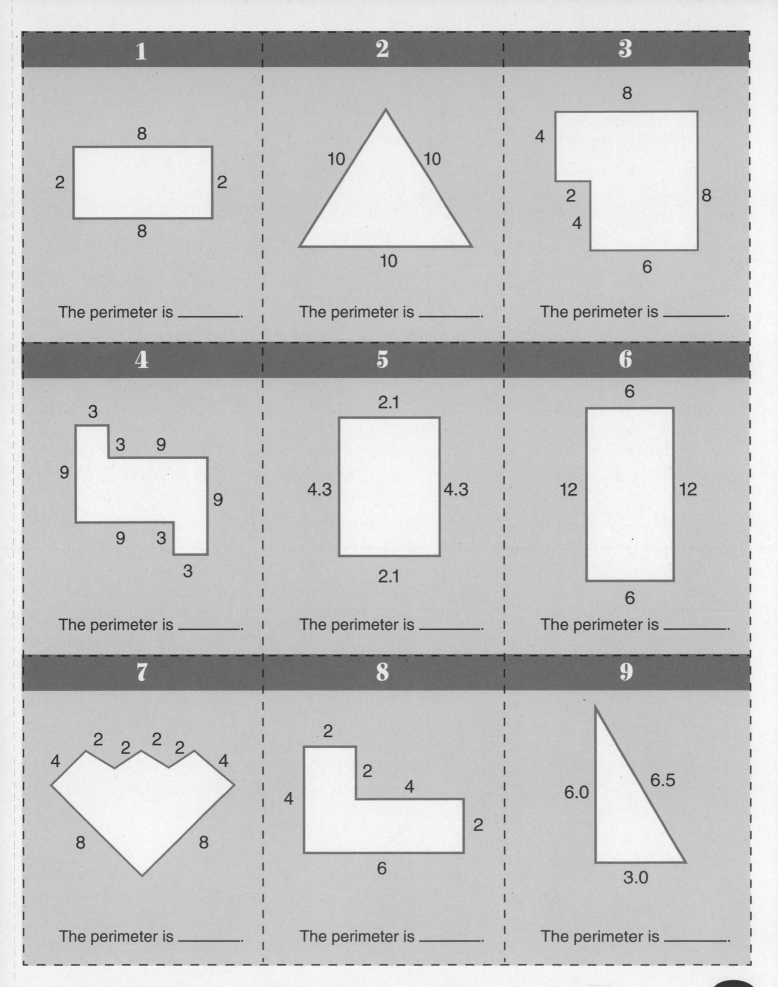

1

8

2   2

8

The perimeter is _____.

2

10   10

10

The perimeter is _____.

3

8

4

2

4

8

6

The perimeter is _____.

4

3

3   9

9

9

9

9   3

3

The perimeter is _____.

5

2.1

4.3   4.3

2.1

The perimeter is _____.

6

6

12   12

6

The perimeter is _____.

7

4   2   2   2   2   4

8   8

The perimeter is _____.

8

2

2

4

4

2

6

The perimeter is _____.

9

6.0   6.5

3.0

The perimeter is _____.

Perimeter and Area

Set 1

Perimeter and Area

Set 1

Perimeter and Area

Set 1

Perimeter and Area

Set 1

Perimeter and Area

Set 1

Perimeter and Area

Set 1

Perimeter and Area

Set 1

Perimeter and Area

Set 1

Perimeter and Area

Set 1

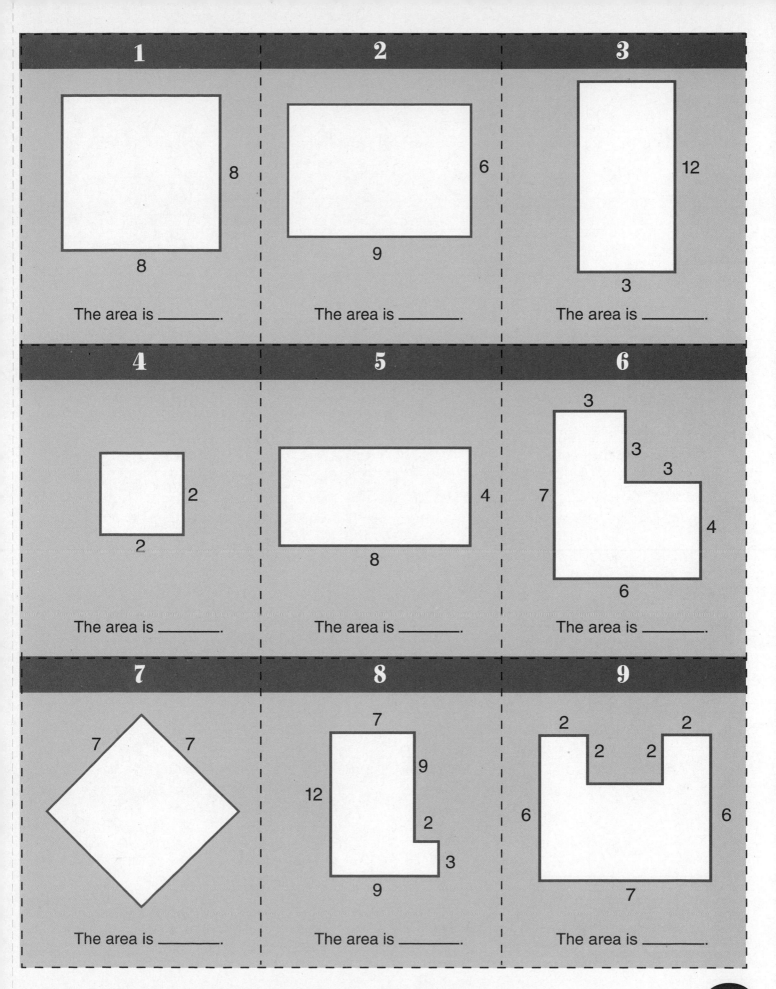

1

8

8

The area is _____.

2

6

9

The area is _____.

3

12

3

The area is _____.

4

2

2

The area is _____.

5

4

8

The area is _____.

6

3

3

3

7

4

6

The area is _____.

7

7   7

The area is _____.

8

7

9

12

2

3

9

The area is _____.

9

2   2

2   2

6   6

7

The area is _____.

Perimeter and Area

Set 2

Perimeter and Area

Set 2

Perimeter and Area

Set 2

Perimeter and Area

Set 2

Perimeter and Area

Set 2

Perimeter and Area

Set 2

Perimeter and Area

Set 2

Perimeter and Area

Set 2

Perimeter and Area

Set 2

Transformations

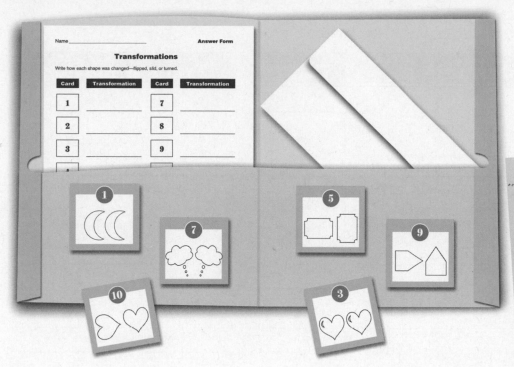

Preparing the Center

1. Prepare a folder following the directions on page 3.

   Cover—page 165
   Student Directions—page 167
   Shape Cards—page 169

2. Reproduce a supply of the answer form on page 164. Place copies in the left-hand pocket of the folder.

Using the Center

1. The student takes the set of shape cards and an answer form.

2. The student selects a card.

3. Next, the student decides if the first shape was flipped, slid, or turned to its new position.

4. The student then writes the answer next to the card number on the answer form.

5. The student identifies the change in position of the remaining shapes.

Transformations

Write how each shape was changed—flipped, slid, or turned.

Card	Transformation	Card	Transformation
1	_____	7	_____
2	_____	8	_____
3	_____	9	_____
4	_____	10	_____
5	_____	11	_____
6	_____	12	_____

Bonus: Draw a heart shape.

Draw it three more times.

1. Flip (reflect) the heart.
2. Slide (translate) the heart.
3. Turn (rotate) the heart.

Transformations

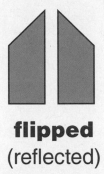

flipped
(reflected)

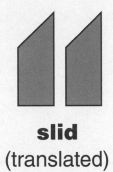

slid
(translated)

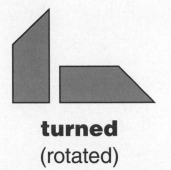

turned
(rotated)

Follow these steps:

1. Take the shape cards and an answer form.

2. Select a card.

3. Decide how the shape was changed (flipped, slid, or turned). Write the answer next to the card's number.

4. Follow Steps 2 and 3 with the remaining shapes.

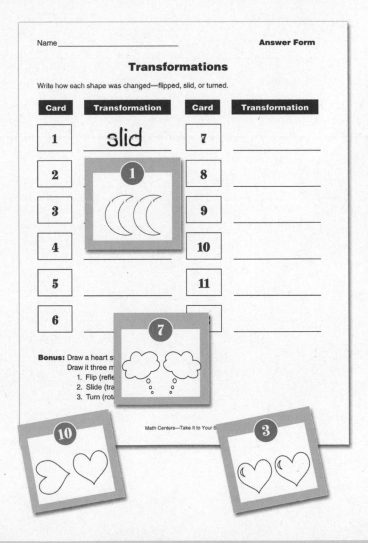

= × ÷

1 5 ∨

0 ∧

÷

7 9 3

∧

6 +

=

2 4

8 × ÷

Transformations

Transformations

Transformations

Transformations

Transformations

Transformations

Transformations

Transformations

Transformations

Transformations

Transformations

Transformations

Pattern Puzzles

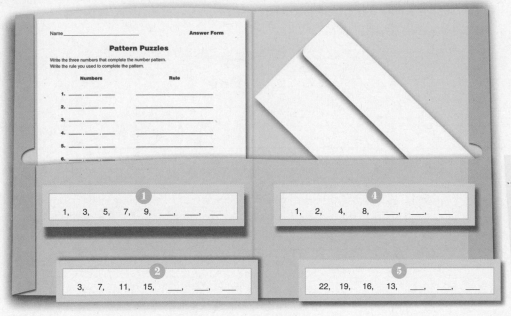

Preparing the Center

1. Prepare a folder following the directions on page 3.

   Cover—page 173
   Student Directions—page 175
   Number Pattern Cards—pages 177, 179

2. Reproduce a supply of the answer form on page 172. Place copies in the left-hand pocket of the folder.

Using the Center

1. The student takes the number pattern cards and the answer form.

2. The student reads one card at a time.

3. Next, the student determines what the next three numbers in the pattern will be and writes them on the lines on the answer form next to the correct card number.

4. The student then writes the rule he or she followed to complete the pattern.

5. The student repeats Steps 2–4 with the other cards.

Name_____   **Answer Form**

Pattern Puzzles

Write the three numbers that complete the number pattern.
Write the rule you used to complete the pattern.

| **Numbers** | **Rule** |

1. ____ , ____ , ____   _____

2. ____ , ____ , ____   _____

3. ____ , ____ , ____   _____

4. ____ , ____ , ____   _____

5. ____ , ____ , ____   _____

6. ____ , ____ , ____   _____

7. ____ , ____ , ____   _____

8. ____ , ____ , ____   _____

9. ____ , ____ , ____   _____

10. ____ , ____ , ____   _____

11. ____ , ____ , ____   _____

12. ____ , ____ , ____   _____

Bonus: On the back of this form, write new number patterns. Write the rule you followed to make each of your patterns.

Math Centers—Take It to Your Seat • EMC 3022 • ©2004 by Evan-Moor Corp.

Pattern Puzzles

Follow these steps:

1. Take the number pattern cards and an answer form.

2. Read one card at a time.

3. Decide what the next three numbers in the pattern will be. Write those numbers on the lines next to the correct card number.

4. Write the rule you followed to find the pattern.

5. Repeat Steps 2–4 with the other cards.

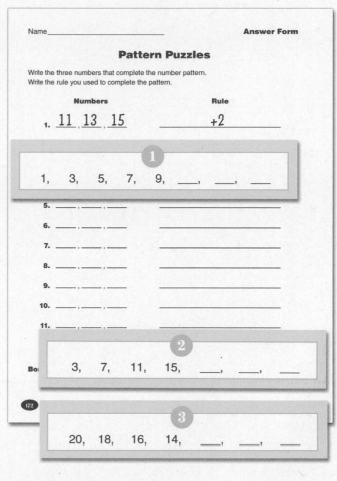

Pattern Puzzles

Write the three numbers that complete the number pattern.
Write the rule you used to complete the pattern.

Numbers	Rule
1. 11 , 13 , 15	+2

1

1, 3, 5, 7, 9, ___, ___, ___

5. ___ , ___ , ___

6. ___ , ___ , ___

7. ___ , ___ , ___

8. ___ , ___ , ___

9. ___ , ___ , ___

10. ___ , ___ , ___

11. ___ , ___ , ___

2

3, 7, 11, 15, ___, ___, ___

3

20, 18, 16, 14, ___, ___, ___

4

1, 2, 4, 8, ___, ___, ___

The rule is count by 3s.

1

1,   3,   5,   7,   9,   ___,   ___,   ___

2

3,   7,   11,   15,   ___,   ___,   ___

3

20,   18,   16,   14,   ___,   ___,   ___

4

1,   2,   4,   8,   ___,   ___,   ___

5

3,   13,   23,   33,   ___,   ___,   ___

6

22,   19,   16,   13,   ___,   ___,   ___

Pattern Puzzles

EMC 3022
©2004 by Evan-Moor Corp

Pattern Puzzles

EMC 3022
©2004 by Evan-Moor Corp

Pattern Puzzles

EMC 3022
©2004 by Evan-Moor Corp

Pattern Puzzles

EMC 3022
©2004 by Evan-Moor Corp

Pattern Puzzles

EMC 3022
©2004 by Evan-Moor Corp

Pattern Puzzles

EMC 3022
©2004 by Evan-Moor Corp

7

5,   11,   17,   23,   ___,   ___,   ___

8

64,   32,   16,   8,   ___,   ___,   ___

9

729,   243,   81,   27,   ___,   ___,   ___

10

52,   60,   68,   76,   ___,   ___,   ___

11

3,   6,   12,   24,   48,   ___,   ___,   ___

12

1,   3,   9,   27,   ___,   ___,   ___

Pattern Puzzles

EMC 3022
©2004 by Evan-Moor Corp

Pattern Puzzles

EMC 3022
©2004 by Evan-Moor Corp

Pattern Puzzles

EMC 3022
©2004 by Evan-Moor Corp

Pattern Puzzles

EMC 3022
©2004 by Evan-Moor Corp

Pattern Puzzles

EMC 3022
©2004 by Evan-Moor Corp

Pattern Puzzles

EMC 3022
©2004 by Evan-Moor Corp

Solid Shapes

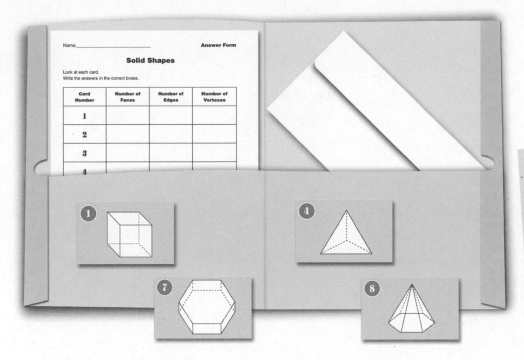

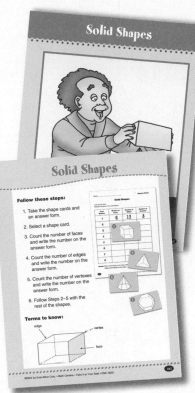

Preparing the Center

1. Prepare a folder following the directions on page 3.

   Cover—page 183
   Student Directions—page 185
   Shape Cards—page 187

2. Reproduce a supply of the answer form on page 182. Place copies in the left-hand pocket of the folder.

Using the Center

1. The student takes the shape cards and an answer form.

2. The student selects a card.

3. Next, the student counts the number of faces, edges, and vertexes and writes them on the answer form.

4. The student continues with the remaining task cards.

Solid Shapes

Look at each card.
Write the answers in the correct boxes.

Card Number	Number of Faces	Number of Edges	Number of Vertexes
1			
2			
3			
4			
5			
6			
7			
8			

Bonus: Draw a solid shape on the back of this form. Write the number of faces, edges, and vertexes that are on your shape.

Solid Shapes

Solid Shapes

Follow these steps:

1. Take the shape cards and an answer form.

2. Select a shape card.

3. Count the number of faces and write the number on the answer form.

4. Count the number of edges and write the number on the answer form.

5. Count the number of vertexes and write the number on the answer form.

6. Follow Steps 2–5 with the rest of the shapes.

Name_____   Answer Form

Solid Shapes

Look at each card.
Write the answers in the correct boxes.

Card Number	Number of Faces	Number of Edges	Number of Vertexes
1	6	12	8
2			
3			
4			
5			
6			
7			
8			

Bonus: Draw a solid shape on the back of this edges, and vertexes on your shape.

182   Math Centers—Take It to Your Seat • EMC 3022 • ©2004 by Evan-Moor Corp.

Terms to know:

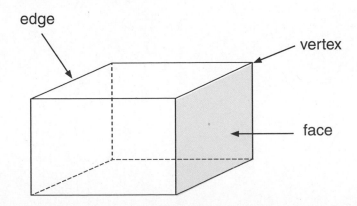

edge

vertex

face

Math Centers—Take It to Your Seat • EMC 3022 • ©2004 by Evan-Moor Corp.

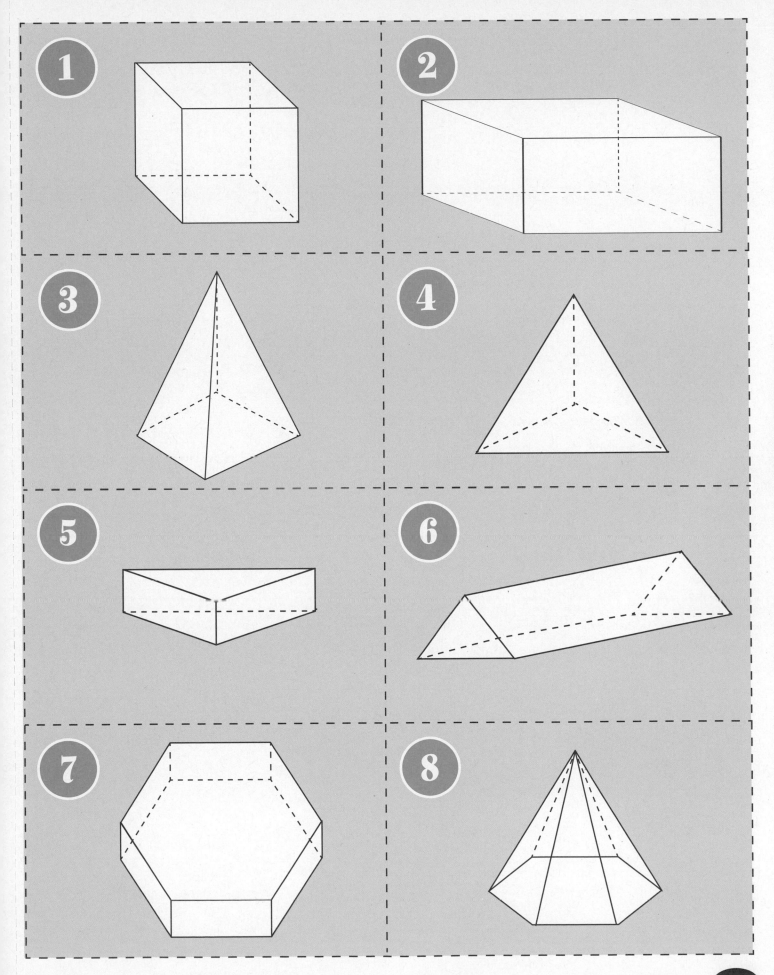

Solid Shapes

EMC 3022
©2004 by Evan-Moor Corp.

Solid Shapes

EMC 3022
©2004 by Evan-Moor Corp.

Solid Shapes

EMC 3022
©2004 by Evan-Moor Corp.

Solid Shapes

EMC 3022
©2004 by Evan-Moor Corp.

Solid Shapes

EMC 3022
©2004 by Evan-Moor Corp.

Solid Shapes

EMC 3022
©2004 by Evan-Moor Corp.

Solid Shapes

EMC 3022
©2004 by Evan-Moor Corp.

Solid Shapes

EMC 3022
©2004 by Evan-Moor Corp.

Answer Key

Money Match—Page 5

Answers may be in a different order.

$0.75—cards 1, 15	$2.80—cards 9, 24
$0.98—cards 5, 20	$4.25—cards 6, 16
$1.25—cards 3, 21	$5.93—cards 11, 23
$1.38—cards 2, 17	$9.00—cards 7, 19
$1.72—cards 10, 22	$12.55—cards 8, 18
$3.12—cards 4, 13	$15.00—cards 12, 14

Bonus: Answers will vary, but must all equal $20.00.

Time Marches On—Page 23

Set 1

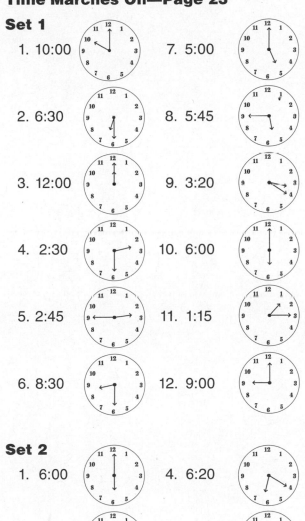

1. 10:00   7. 5:00

2. 6:30   8. 5:45

3. 12:00   9. 3:20

4. 2:30   10. 6:00

5. 2:45   11. 1:15

6. 8:30   12. 9:00

Set 2

1. 6:00   4. 6:20

2. 8:35   5. 12:25

3. 7:00   6. 2:05

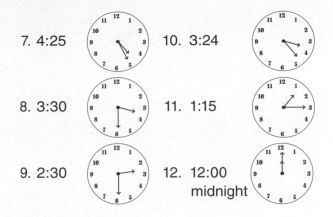

7. 4:25   10. 3:24

8. 3:30   11. 1:15

9. 2:30   12. 12:00 midnight

Bonus: Answers will vary.

Fill It Up!—Page 37

Answers may be in a different order.

Set 1	Set 2
1 pint = 2 cups	3 cups = 24 ounces
1 quart = 2 pints	1½ cups = 12 ounces
1 gallon = 4 quarts	½ gallon = 4 pints
8 ounces = 1 cup	6 cups = 1½ quarts
½ cup = 4 ounces	16 ounces = 1 pint
2 ounces = ¼ cup	32 ounces = 1 quart
½ gallon = 2 quarts	1 gallon = 8 pints
2 gallons = 8 quarts	3 pints = 6 cups

Bonus: Answers will vary, but answers must equal one gallon.

Number Square Puzzler—Page 53

*The numbers in these problems can be reversed and still be correct.

1.

	*	*
9	7	6
+ 4	+ 8	+ 5
1 3	15	11
1 0	*	8
+ 2		+ 6
12		1 4

2.

1 2	1 6	11
– 8	– 9	– 5
4	7	6
1 3	14	10
– 3	– 6	– 9
1 0	8	1

3.

5	8	3
× [5]	× 4	× [3]
2 5	3 [2]	9

[8]	[7]	[6]
× 5	× 3	× 8
4 [0]	2 1	[4] 8

4.

$$9\overline{)4\,[5]}\quad\quad [9]\atop 6\overline{)54}$$

$$*\,[7]\atop 3\overline{)21}\quad\quad [5]\atop 6\overline{)3\,0}$$

$$[1]\,2\atop 4\overline{)48}\quad\quad *\,[8]\atop 2\overline{)16}$$

Bonus: Answers will vary, but numbers 0–9 can be used as missing numbers only one time each.

Read a Graph—Page 69

Graph 1
1. bar
2. Answers will vary.
3. 5 more
4. Maria
5. Raul

Graph 2
1. line
2. Answers will vary.
3. 75°
4. 1:00 P.M., 90°
5. 5° cooler

Graph 3
1. circle
2. Answers will vary.
3. jelly beans—He bought more jelly beans than any other type of candy.
4. jelly beans
5. hard candies

Graph 4
1. bar
2. 1 person
3. 17 slices
4. 6 slices
5. The numbers show the number of slices of pizza that were eaten.

Graph 5
1. bar
2. 20 children
3. 25 children
4. 10 more children
5. dodge ball

Graph 6
1. bar
2. boys
3. 5 more boys
4. more girls, 4 more
5. Room 9, 8 girls

The bonus answer for each graph will vary, but there must be two questions that can be correctly answered by reading the graph.

Make a Graph—Page 81

1.

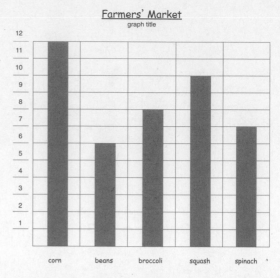

2.

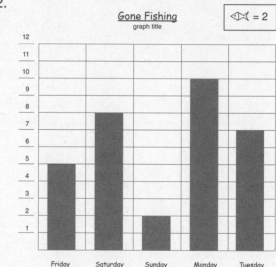

3.

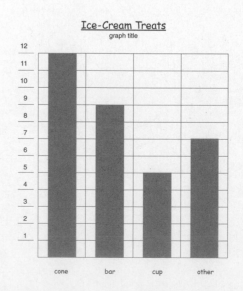

4.

How Do You Get to School?
graph title

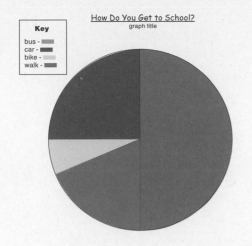

Key
bus -
car -
bike -
walk -

5.

What's the Temperature?
graph title

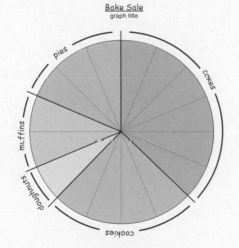

6.

Bake Sale
graph title

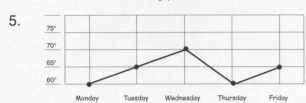

7.

Wonder World
graph title

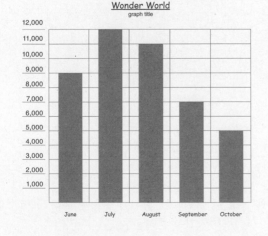

8.

Super Shoe Sale
graph title

George -
Marge -

The bonus answer for each graph will vary, but there must be three questions that can be correctly answered by reading the graph.

How Many Combinations?—Page 93
Answers may be in a different order.

Shirt	Pants	Shirt	Pants
white	red	red	white
white	blue	red	black
white	white	blue	red
white	black	blue	blue
red	red	blue	white
red	blue	blue	black

Bonus: 20 combinations

Name That Part!—Page 103
Answers may be in a different order.

Set 1

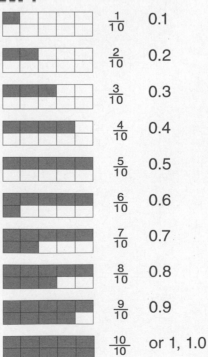

$\frac{1}{10}$ 0.1

$\frac{2}{10}$ 0.2

$\frac{3}{10}$ 0.3

$\frac{4}{10}$ 0.4

$\frac{5}{10}$ 0.5

$\frac{6}{10}$ 0.6

$\frac{7}{10}$ 0.7

$\frac{8}{10}$ 0.8

$\frac{9}{10}$ 0.9

$\frac{10}{10}$ or 1, 1.0

Set 2

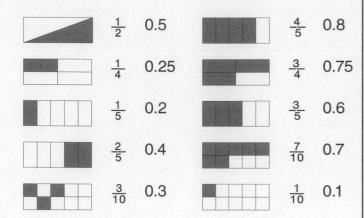

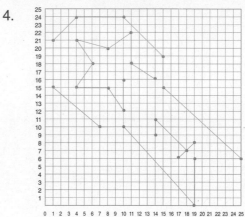

Plotting a Picture—Page 121

1.
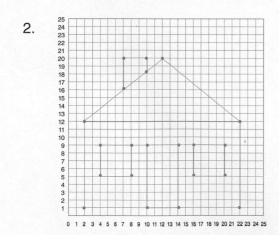

2.
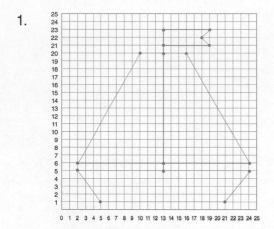

3.
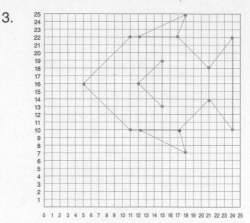

4.
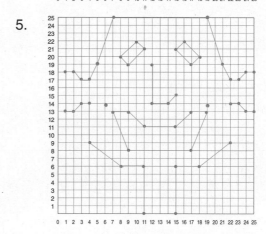

5.
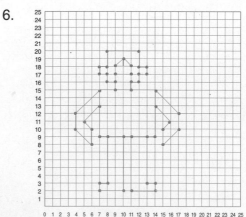

6.

Bonus: Pictures will vary, but must follow the rules for an ordered-pair picture.

Math Centers—Take It to Your Seat • EMC 3022 • ©2004 by Evan-Moor Corp.